Uncooking With RawRose

(Your Guide To Raw Foods)

By Rose Vasile

ACKNOWLEDGEMENTS

Writing this book has made me realize how fortunate I am. Many wonderful people have given freely of their time to edit the book, provide advice, lots of encouragement and share my excitement. Thanks and lots of hugs to everyone!

I want to acknowledge some special contributions:

My daughter Lisa for being a sounding board for my ideas, for reassuring me when I wondered what I was doing writing a book, and for giving me wonderful hugs and back rubs.

Friends who edited my book, giving me great feedback and comments: Ray Bacon, Rachel Cunnington, Kristi Inman, Bruce Melville, Pat Newson, Jody Trigg and Dale Marie Young. Special thanks to Pat Newson, who put a lot of energy into providing excellent feedback, after she thoroughly researched the subjects.

Victoria Boutenko for editing my manuscript and writing a wonderful Foreword, for teaching me how to prepare tasty foods, for being my inspiration and a special friend on my raw journey.

Janette Murray-Wakelin and Alan Murray, owners of ZenZero-The Secret of Health, for their support and for giving me the opportunity to encourage people to live healthier lifestyles.

Aurel Vasile for his help and patience teaching me how to use a digital camera.

Stephen Cochrane and Ray Kent for freely sharing their wisdom about raw foods and fasting.

Linda Magnuson for her suggestions about book publishing and for her encouragement.

TABLE OF CONTENTS

Chapter 5 – APPETIZERS, CRACKERS, SALADS, ENTREES

FOREWORD

Rose Vasile's book is a gift to all of us. It is a practical and easy-to-follow guide for making a wide variety of delicious raw foods. I am privileged to know Rose personally. When Rose came to one of my classes about six years ago, I instantly spotted her shy, smiley face and her keen interest in anything about raw foods. Since then, we have become good friends.

To me, Rose is one of the best organized and most hardworking individuals on the planet. Hence, we are fortunate to have her recipe book with extremely accurate, pre-measured, and pre-tested instructions that guarantee a scrumptious taste.

With the author's simple, down-to-earth explanations, this book is especially helpful for beginners to raw food. At the same time, the abundance of recipes will easily attract longtime raw fooders.

Rose's sincere style, combined with her personal story, makes the reading engaging. The book's appendix contains a helpful wellness assessment based on the author's personal "raw" journey. I envision the dining experiences of many families will be illuminated, in many ways, by the use of Rose's wonderful book.

Victoria Boutenko
November 2006
Author of
Green for Life,
12 Steps to Raw Foods
and *Raw Family*

EDITORS' COMMENTS

Bravo Rose! Uncooking With Raw Rose is the first raw foods book from our thriving raw foods community in the Comox Valley (Vancouver Island, Canada). I am impressed with the fact that Rose uses all raw ingredients, along with explanations about some controversial ones. The recipes are easy to follow, with techniques and ingredients that make fabulous food. The Amazing Avocados are perfect; the Pizzas—including Barbeque Sauce, Marinated Mushrooms and Pizza Crust—are the best I've ever tasted; and the Truffles are divinely decadent! This book makes a raw diet palatable and achievable for all of us.

Pat Newson

Having been a raw fooder for two years, I found *Uncooking With RawRose* to be truly inspirational and informative. It is presented in a simplistic and useful fashion that makes the transition to raw foods easy for anyone. Rose's recipes are delicious and easy to integrate into any lifestyle. Enjoy the uncooking and the good health that will follow.

Rachel Cunnington

As a budding raw foodist, with infrequent uncooking experience, I was compelled to read Rose's book. I'm delighted by it. It's a liberating cornucopia of informative, yet simple recipes. I'll keep a copy in my kitchen for years to come. Thank you Rose!

Ray Bacon

Rose's book is very informative, well written, and laid out. I can't wait to make some of the recipes. There is something for everyone. I never knew that there is such a wide variety of foods you can make. I would suggest this book to everyone. It's fun to read, interesting, and has a lot of stuff everybody should know. ROSE ROCKS!!!

Kristi Inman

Rose's story is very inspiring; recipes and methods are very clear and mouth-watering. *Uncooking With RawRose* has provided me with the knowledge to go into the "raw" world full of confidence. The colourful photos of raw foods will inspire me even more!

Jody Trigg

Thank you Rose for your commitment to raw foods. You have inspired me to eat more raw plant foods and I look forward to trying your raw recipes. You convinced me that raw foods are the best thing for my physical and mental health. Raw is law! Many happy meals to you in the future.

Bruce Melville,
Fellow Raw Foodist

When I first went "100% raw" in 2004, I took Rose's "Uncooking Classes". The tips and recipes I learned (all of which are now in this book) were invaluable to me. Her recipes made going raw extremely easy. Today her recipes continue to inspire my commitment to a raw diet and are always a favourite at any potluck!!

Dale Marie Young,
Raw Lifestyle Coach

CHAPTER 1 - INTRODUCTION

Congratulations! You're one of the fortunate people who've heard about the benefits of raw foods and are interested in getting on the road to vibrant health! This book was written to make it easier for you to add more raw vegan foods to your diet. My goal is to provide you with simple, tasty recipes that are truly raw and to give you information that will make your transition smoother.

Years from now, I don't want you to look back and ask:

WAS RAW FOOD THE ANSWER TO MY DISEASE (ALLERGIES, ARTHRITIS, CANCER, CELIAC, CHRONIC FATIGUE, DIABETES, HIGH BLOOD PRESSURE, HIGH CHOLESTEROL, IRRITABLE BOWEL SYNDROME, M.S., OBESITY, PARKINSON'S, ETC.....) BUT I DIDN'T GIVE IT A TRY?

MY STORY

I was born in Kitchener, Ontario, Canada on October 13, 1951. As far back as I can remember, I've had a problem with my weight. Throughout my childhood, I was about fifteen pounds overweight. Compared to the obesity of a lot of children today, fifteen pounds may not sound like a huge amount, but it was enough to make me self-conscious at a time when most children were fit. Mom was a great cook. We enjoyed a lot of breaded meats, cabbage rolls and cold deli meats. Vegetables were usually cooked with a cream sauce, or even breaded, although I also remember tasty salads. Grandma was a fantastic baker, making mouth-watering strudels, tortes and cookies. No one ever had to tell me about the starving children in Africa to convince me to finish a meal. In fact, sometimes I complained because I didn't get as much food as my Dad! When I was about eight years old, Mom took me to the doctor to put me on a diet. I don't recall losing much weight.

As a child, I was usually severely constipated. I can't imagine it now, but it was quite normal for me to go for a week or even two weeks without having a bowel movement! I was often given a laxative to help move things along.

When I was twelve, smoking (cigarettes) was the "cool" thing to do when parents weren't around. By the time I was fifteen, I was smoking almost a pack a day. As an adult, I tried quitting many times: on my own, with a friend, on a bet, New Year's resolutions, using the nicotine patch, and taking various smoke-ending courses. Each time I quit, I replaced cigarettes with food. Trying to quit always made me feel like a failure, so finally I stopped quitting.

In my adult years I gained and lost weight many times--taking diet pills, using diet products and attending weight loss programs, However, by the time I was 41, my weight was approaching 200 pounds. At that point a friend gave me *Fit For Life* by Harvey & Marilyn Diamond. This book talked about how you could increase your energy by eating only fresh fruits and juices in the morning. Eating fruit in the morning really helped me. I had so much energy! I didn't feel brain dead around mid-morning and my elimination became regular and easier. The book talked about Natural Hygiene, which is mainly about eating raw vegan foods. Natural Hygiene sounded too far out for me to accept, although it planted seeds for the future.

My children, Lisa and Paul, were vegetarians when they were young teenagers. They even tried eating a raw vegan diet for a short while. I was relieved when they stopped eating only raw foods because I was concerned they wouldn't get all the nutrients their growing bodies needed. They often talked about animal rights and gave me the book *Diet For A New America* by John Robbins. The book describes the inhumane and unhealthy conditions factory-farmed animals are subjected to. Breaded veal had been a favourite food in our family, so I was especially moved reading how veal calves are raised. At age 45 I became a vegetarian. People think of vegetarians as slim, but I found lots of sugary and fried foods to enjoy. Becoming vegetarian didn't produce any improvement in the food allergies I had started to acquire when I was 26. In fact, the list of foods I was allergic to grew. Around that time I stopped colouring my hair because of the toxins in hair colouring products.

At age 48 I was ready to quit smoking for the last time. I was feeling tightness in my chest and had trouble taking deep breaths. Also, there was more information in the media regarding how the tobacco industry had known about health concerns of smoking for a long time, yet still promoted smoking. This motivated me to quit. I strongly associated drinking coffee and pop with smoking, so I stopped drinking them. I began walking to replace the smoking habit. I was successful in quitting smoking and drinking caffeine, but within a few weeks my body had very little energy because it wasn't getting the chemicals it was used to. Dr. Ellie Fuke, a Naturopathic Physician, put me on a detoxification diet which included eliminating wheat and sugar. On that diet, my body was able to regain energy within a month. Ellie also advised me that bras, especially tight ones with underwire support, impede the necessary flow of lymph and might contribute to breast cancer. I began wearing camisoles instead of bras.

Along with improvements in my health from the changes I had made, my confidence improved. **Each time I accomplished something I thought I couldn't do, fears became easier to overcome!** It gave me the courage to move from Kitchener, Ontario, where I had lived all my life, to Vancouver, British Columbia. Also, I stopped wearing makeup in order to be more real, and due to concerns about the safety of most cosmetics.

When I was 49, my daughter, Lisa was again an example for me. She ate only raw foods for four months and lost weight. I was very interested and in January 2001 began attending raw potlucks and took some raw food preparation classes. As I increased my consumption of raw foods,

I found that, besides easily losing over fifty pounds, eating raw foods provided these benefits for me:
- more energy
- improved mental clarity and concentration
- allergies disappeared (23 years of food allergies and three year allergy to latex)
- improved complexion (good colour, smoother texture)
- eyes looked younger and more vibrant--not puffy with dark circles
- improved gums (previously I had gum disease and my front teeth had been shifting)
- improved elimination and reduction in hemorrhoids
- fewer mood swings
- no heartburn and indigestion
- my hunger was satisfied and intense food cravings disappeared
- mosquitoes stopped biting
- didn't need deodorant anymore
- chronic joint stiffness of my right ankle disappeared
- needed less sleep, so I had more free time

In 2001 I met Victoria Boutenko and her wonderful family. Fourteen years ago, the Boutenkos changed to 100% raw foods in order to eliminate their son's juvenile diabetes. As a result, Victoria's husband's arthritis and thyroid problems, and their daughter's chronic asthma went away. Victoria's heart arrhythmia disappeared, along with over 100 pounds of excess weight. Besides reading her excellent books about raw foods (see **www.rawfamily.com**), I've heard Victoria speak many times and her sincere, enlightened presentations continue to inspire me. I graduated from the Raw Family's 'Raw Living Foods Chef' course offered in 2002 in Ashland, Oregon.

For 31 years I was an underwriter of group life and health insurance. A major focus of health insurance is paying drug claims. After eating raw foods for two years, I was convinced that drugs weren't the answer to most of our health problems. They only relieve the symptoms, but don't correct the problem. In fact, the side effects of drugs often make people sicker. Rather than working in an industry concerned with paying for drugs, I decided to put my energy into inspiring people to heal with raw foods. At Victoria Boutenko's suggestion, I quit my job as underwriting manager and went to Creative Health Institute (CHI) in Michigan, USA to learn all I could about raw foods. CHI runs two week cleansing programs based on Dr. Ann Wigmore's teachings, emphasizing eating raw foods and wheatgrass juice. I became the Director of CHI, which was a great learning experience.

Four years ago I moved to lovely Courtenay on Vancouver Island, British Columbia. Here, an ever-increasing number of people are turning to raw foods as the answer to their health challenges. For two and a half years I had fun working at ZenZero-the Secret of Health. I assisted many wonderful people in ZenZero's unique vegan restaurant which provides raw foods, and in the store which sells products for a healthy raw lifestyle. I was the coordinator of ZenZero Centre for Optimum Health, which provides holistic health education, and I continue to teach raw food classes there. I also travel to various communities where I teach raw food classes, give raw food demonstrations and meet lots of interesting people.

I've written this book to share some of the knowledge I've acquired in seven years of eating mainly raw foods, and hopefully to inspire you to be the best you can be!

YOUR STORY?

Following is an inspiring Health Survey created by Frederic Patenaude (see **www.fredericpatenaude.com** for great raw information) which shows the most common benefits people experience when they eat raw foods. See how many of these statements are part of your story:

*- You have amazing **energy**. You wake up in the morning ready to go, and you rarely feel ups and downs in your energy during the day.*

*- Your **skin** looks great. People often comment how clear your skin is.*

*- You're at your ideal **weight**. Your friends admire you and ask you what kind of diet you follow.*

*- You don't feel deprived when eating. You can **eat as much as you want** and not gain weight.*

*- You fall asleep easily. You rarely suffer from insomnia. Your **sleep** is deep and sound.*

*- You have **regular** bowel movements and rarely experience constipation or indigestion.*

*- You **look younger** than most people your age.*

*- You have greater than average **fitness** even when you don't exercise regularly.*

*- Your **eyes** are clear and bright. People often comment on how bright your eyes are.*

*- You feel **happy** for no reason. You don't need coffee to stimulate you or alcohol to make you laugh. You are never depressed.*

*- You can easily **focus** and concentrate for long hours without feeling tired.*

*- You are in touch with your **intuition**. You "instinctively" know when something is good for you.*

ABOUT RAW

As the health of many North Americans declines, people are searching for solutions. A growing number are finding that eating raw foods can have dramatic results. I know it sounds almost too simple, but **YOU'LL SEE A NOTICEABLE IMPROVEMENT IN YOUR VITALITY JUST BY EATING MAINLY RAW VEGAN FOODS.**

'Raw food' normally refers to vegan food that hasn't been heated above 105 degrees Fahrenheit (40.6 Celsius). It's food that contains the nutrients and enzymes our body needs to thrive. Raw food consists of fruits, vegetables, especially greens, nuts, seeds, grains and some fermented foods, including red wine. Vegan is food free of all animal products, including eggs, dairy, honey and gelatin.

Do you know of any other animal that cooks its food? Heating food at temperatures above 105 degrees changes the chemistry of the food, destroying the food's vitality. Eating raw food helps our body detoxify, then rebuild using the materials we need. There's truth to the expression **"You are what you eat"**.

People who eat raw foods as 75% or more of their diet are often referred to as 'raw fooders'. Among raw fooders, there are different beliefs about what the ideal diet looks like. No one knows what the "perfect" diet is, and it may be somewhat different for everyone. Victoria Boutenko's research into the appropriate foods for humans makes sense. In her book *Green for Life*, Victoria suggests that raw fooders increase greens and reduce fats. I try to eat a raw food diet of 50% fruits, 40% greens and other vegetables, and 10% fats.
- Fruits are cleansing and the best source of carbohydrates, vitamins and water.
- Greens and other vegetables are high in proteins, minerals, vitamins and fiber and help stabilize blood sugar.
- Fats lubricate the body and slow sugar absorption.

It's best to limit the amount of nuts, seeds and oils we eat. Our ancestors had to manually crack nuts. As a result, they didn't eat many at a time, compared with the way we grab a handful of nuts to munch on. Seeds have less fat than nuts, so are the preferred choice.

One of the first questions people usually ask about eating raw foods is "Where do you get your protein?" Consider a cow. It grows very large eating greens. The cow takes amino acids from greens and joins them into the protein molecules it needs. When we eat meat, our body needs to break down the meat's protein molecules into simple amino acids, then reformat them into the protein our body needs. This is a lot of work for our digestive system. Why not cut out the middleman and eat greens rather than meat? We can obtain adequate protein by eating greens. Our bodies will thank us, as well as the animals. When I eat green, leafy vegetables, I feel more vibrant.

Our body's ideal alkaline to acid ratio is 80% alkaline and 20% acidic. An acidic body is oxygen depleted, which makes it a breeding ground for all disease. The chlorophyll in green leafy vegetables is liquid oxygen. Here is a rough breakdown of foods:

ACID FORMING FOODS:
- meat, including fish and poultry
- dairy and eggs
- grains
- sugar
- cooked food
- unsoaked nuts and seeds, except almonds
- alcohol

ALKALINE FORMING FOODS:
- raw vegetables, especially green leafy vegetables
- ripe raw fruit
- soaked and sprouted nuts and seeds

On a raw food diet we don't need to drink much water because fruits and vegetables contain lots of water. We need more water if we're eating dehydrated foods, salty foods or doing lots of exercise. Drinking water with a raw meal dilutes the digestive enzymes.

I believe that taking supplements may put our body out of balance. Try to eat an assortment of foods in order to obtain all the nutrients we require.

Often people say they need a hot meal in the winter to keep them warm. Here's part of a good explanation Victoria Boutenko provides as to why eating a hot meal is detrimental to your health:

"Would a quarter pound of rice physically keep a 160 pound body warm? In order to get warmed by it, one would have to fill a bathtub with warm rice and sit in it for 20 minutes. So why do we feel warmer after consuming cooked food?...When any impure substances get into our blood through the walls of the intestines, they irritate our adrenals......The adrenals immediately begin to produce....hormones which stimulate our sympathetic nervous system, which is why we feel awake at first. They also force our heart to beat faster and to pump larger amounts of blood through our body, which makes us feel warm. This feeling doesn't last long and we pay a high price for it. After 10-15 minutes our body gets exhausted from performing extra work, the heart requires rest, the nervous system becomes inhibited, and we feel tired, sleepy and even colder than before. However, we remember only the feeling of getting warmer after eating cooked food....This harmful practice wears the body out and by the end of the winter many people feel exhausted and depleted......weakened adrenals eventually won't be able to work properly even at warm temperatures. For example, most older people feel cold even in the middle of the summer...
...During your first raw winter you may experience some cold due to the weakened adrenals, so put on an extra sweater, take a hot bath, or do some pushups. If you will continue staying raw, your adrenals will rest and recover, your capillary circulation will improve, your nervous system and your heart will naturally strengthen without any artificial stimulation. In a year you will tolerate cold better than ever before...."

People going on a raw food diet usually lose weight because raw foods are nutritionally dense, yet low in calories. Our body doesn't need to work hard to digest foods, so we have more energy. Gradually toxins and fats stored in our cells are cleaned out. The body rebuilds cells using healthy materials from raw foods. As a result, the body naturally finds its ideal weight - people who are overweight lose weight; whereas those who are too slim gain weight.

Any change requires a period of adjustment; therefore, most people make a gradual move to eating raw foods. Many will never move to a totally raw diet. As you eat more raw foods, you'll enjoy improved health and will probably want to eat fewer cooked foods.

CHAPTER 2 - LET'S GET STARTED!

When I adventured into raw foods seven years ago, I was anxious to get started, but became confused about how to do it properly. I knew I wouldn't be using my stove, but wondered if I should buy a food processor (yes), a better blender (would be ideal) and a juicer (not necessary). Each answer seemed to lead to another question. My goal is to give you information to make your raw journey easier. Now let's get started!

MAKING RAW WORK FOR YOU!

When you were born you didn't know how to prepare cooked foods—you had to learn. Preparing raw foods is easier than preparing cooked foods, but initially there's a period of adjustment as you learn some of the basics. After a while you'll be changing recipes to suit your preferences and inventing your own recipes.

Start by making a list of the foods and recipes you eat that are raw, or ones that need minor changes to be raw (e.g. fruits, fruit salads, fresh juices, sprouts, salads, guacamole, salsa, veggies for dips...). If you have some favourite cooked recipes, you may be able to modify them into raw recipes.

At first people usually prepare raw food recipes that remind them of cooked foods. They want foods with lots of flavour from spices, salt and natural sweeteners. Also they use a lot of oil and fats to get that satisfied feeling. After a while they simplify their eating and listen to what their body is asking for.

Most of us don't eat enough greens. An easy and tasty way to include more raw foods in your diet is to make Green Smoothies. In your blender, combine about 60% fruits and water, with 40% greens. With all the fruit, the Smoothie won't taste "green". Vary the types of fruits and greens you use so that your body gets the nutrients it needs.

See Chapter 3 for more Smoothie ideas. Having a blended drink is a quick easy way to get energy because your body doesn't need to work hard to digest the food.

Forget about the foods you normally eat for breakfast, lunch or supper. You can have Smoothies for breakfast, or any time of the day. Contrary to advertising, you don't need to count calories and you don't need to have three meals a day. Just listen to the messages your body sends you, which will vary based on your level of activity from day to day. If you're hungry, eat. If you're not hungry, don't eat. Try not to eat at least two to three hours before going to sleep, otherwise it may be harder to fall asleep and your sleep won't be as deep.

I always eat fruit in the morning, whether it's in a Green Smoothie or just eating the fruit whole. It gives me so much energy, that I'm not attracted to other foods. For the first year of eating raw I felt best when I had lunch around 1:30, then didn't feel like eating a big meal in the evening. Lunch was usually a salad, veggies and dip, or Veggie Pate rolled in greens with crackers on the side. For supper I often had a soup and/or treats such as macadamia, Brazil or pine nuts, or Ice Creme. I usually had an avocado each day in my soup or salad.

Now I eat simpler, except at weekly raw potlucks, where I enjoy an assortment of wonderfully prepared raw foods. For breakfast/lunch I have about four cups of Green Smoothie or fruits. I find it very satisfying. Supper is usually a Salad (see Salad Ideas), with a treat later.

To make tasty raw foods, familiarize yourself with the Five Tastes (see description in this chapter). Stop using processed salt in your diet. Instead, use natural sea salts and sea vegetables. Dr. Neil Barnard, author of *Turn Off The Fat Genes*, says it takes about three weeks to change your taste genes, which I've found to be true.

Once you're feeling more comfortable with raw foods, consider making a three or six month commitment to eating only raw foods to see what difference it makes to your health. Unless you have a serious illness that needs to be dealt with very quickly, for the first few months, eat in the framework of "Is it raw?" Don't worry about counting calories, proper food combining, the amount of fats you're eating, or even the amount of food. After a while your body will start telling you what it needs.

I truly believe that eating 100% raw is the ideal diet for optimum health. Victoria Boutenko suggests, and I totally agree, that a 100% raw diet is easier for compulsive eaters than 70%, 80% or 90% raw. That's because you don't need to give any attention to cooked foods.

Be aware of the messages you are sending yourself. If you are like me, you constantly have a conversation going on in your head. Make sure you're not beating yourself up. When you tell yourself you can't do something, there's a good chance you won't be able to do it. When someone asks "Is that all you can eat?", tell them you can eat anything you want, but you choose to eat raw foods.

Jim Carey, who produces the online newsletter for Creative Health Institute (**www.chidiet.com/news/**), has some good advice. He says *"Eating outside of the program isn't cheating or failing. You're just making poorer choices about how you eat, you're dealing with addictions to your old comfort foods, and you've simply been eating outside of the program. Remember this is a lifestyle choice, not a religion."*

Each time we accomplish something new, or get over old fears, we build confidence. As a result, the next time we're faced with change it will be easier, and even fun to work through.

After you've been on a raw food diet for a while, try not to overeat. Although overeating raw foods usually doesn't cause weight gain, your body won't be as healthy as possible. Tune into your sense of taste—at the point when your food doesn't taste as good, you know your body has had enough to eat.

Eat a wide variety of foods, food that's in season and, ideally, foods that are locally grown. Try to eat organic food as much as possible.

Never leave home without nibbles such as seeds, fresh or dried fruit, even if you only expect to be gone a short while. Your errand might take longer than anticipated, or you might get hunger pangs when you pass a restaurant you used to enjoy.

When you first 'go raw', getting lots of sleep is important. It helps your body heal. Also, when you are rested, you have more willpower to resist those old cooked food habits. Drinking extra water when you start the raw food diet helps flush out toxins. A glass of water when you wake up aids elimination.

Herbert M. Shelton supported the concept of the Law of Vital Accommodation. This Law asserted that, in order to survive, our body gradually adjusts to toxic substances that it can't eliminate. It insulates itself with mucous, or stores the toxins in our cells. As time passes, our body reacts to the stored toxins and we get cancer, or other diseases. After being on raw foods for a while, a lot of the toxins have been cleansed from our body and we've reduced our tolerance for toxins. Therefore a raw fooder may have a strong reaction to cooked foods, or toxins. I like Shelton's description:

"The more sound and vigorous the organism or any part of it, the more prompt and vigorous will be its action in resisting and expelling a poison of any kind—the more acutely will it feel, the more readily will it resent, and the more violently will it resist and expel the tobacco, alcohol, arsenic or other poison. Try it when, where and with whom you please, you will find no exception to this law of organic life."

When I had been eating 100% raw foods for almost a year and a half, I drank a glass of freshly prepared Nut Mylk that had maple syrup added to it. I wasn't aware that it contained maple syrup, which isn't raw. However, my body knew almost instantly. Within five minutes of drinking the Nut Mylk, I didn't know which end of me it wanted to come out of first! My "violent" reaction (as Shelton put it) lasted for less than an hour, but the reaction was strong enough to expel all traces of the maple syrup.

When you start enjoying the benefits of raw foods, you'll probably want to convince your family and friends that the raw food diet is the way to go. Tell them what you're doing, but be careful not to push it on them. Unfortunately, in our eagerness to share this information with those we care about, we often turn them against raw foods. The foods we choose to eat are usually based on long established habits that give us comfort. Watch that you don't put down their food choices—not only in words, but in the expression on your face when they are eating something you know isn't good for them. Live by example. Offer them some of your Green Smoothie or a dessert creation. After a while they'll notice the improvements in your health and may become interested in trying raw foods. Don't be discouraged.

After eating fruits and sweet treats, it's a good idea to rinse your mouth with water or brush your teeth.

An occasional glass of red wine is OK, but don't overdo it. Wine can lower your willpower to stay on raw foods. Also, the sulphates in most wines aren't good for you, so drink organic, sulphate-free red wine.

When I started eating mainly raw foods, I made a list of the health benefits (physical and emotional) I hoped to enjoy. I put it on the fridge as encouragement for me to make the right food choices. I found that I had to add to the list because there were benefits I hadn't expected. One of the welcome surprises was the healing of chronic joint stiffness in my ankle which I had since I was an adolescent. Review your list from time to time because as our health improves we tend to forget how we were feeling before we started eating raw foods. You'll be more motivated to continue.

A Wellness Assessment and a Diary page are in the Appendix. I encourage you to complete the Wellness Assessment and use the Diary when you start eating raw, or even before you start. Seeing the results will encourage you and make you more aware of potential improvements to your health. The Diary will help you see how sleep, diet and physical activity are affecting you.

YOUR RAW KITCHEN

Eating a raw food diet can be as simple as eating one type of fruit or vegetable, which is referred to as a "mono-meal". However, most people prefer food combinations, especially in the early stages of eating raw foods. Having the right tools and food staples in your kitchen will make raw food preparation easier. Here are the main appliances and tools I have in my kitchen, followed by my kitchen staples:

<u>APPLIANCES & TOOLS:</u>
I had fun trying to put this list in order of importance, considering what is nice to have and what you could get by without.

- CUTTING BOARD

- SHARP KNIFE AND SHARPENING STONE

- BLENDER – A Vita-Mix blender is ideal because it has lots of power and the container holds eight cups. If you don't have a powerful blender, cut fruits and vegetables into small pieces before blending.

- FOOD PROCESSOR – Food processors come in various sizes, from three to fourteen cups. I use the 11 cup size because you can fit the whole recipe in the food processor, instead of doing it in small batches. However, I also have a 3 cup food processor to take along when I travel. Most large food processors also come with a grating and slicing attachment which are wonderful for slicing apples (see Apple Pie recipe) and for grating carrots and beets (see Can't Beet That Salad recipe).

- GRATER – Large holes for carrots, beets, parsnips, celeriac, etc. and small holes for grating lemon zest.

- MIXING BOWLS – Made of glass, ceramic or stainless steel.

- VEGETABLE PEELER – To peel carrots, parsnips, ginger, yams, etc.

- METAL STRAINER - For draining, rinsing and sprouting soaked nuts, seeds and grains. Can also be used to strain Nut Mylk (see recipe), although a Nut Mylk / Sprouting bag works better.

- COFFEE GRINDER – Great for grinding flax seeds, sesame seeds and whole spices. Also good for grinding nuts. To clean, wipe the inside with a dry cloth or use a small brush. Wash the lid. If there's still a coffee drinker in your house, it's nice to have a separate grinder for coffee.

- DEHYDRATOR – Excalibur is the most popular brand. Trays in their four tray models are 12" x 12", and 14" x 14" in their five and nine tray models.
- You'll find other brands that are round with a hole in the middle. Be sure to choose one with an adjustable thermostat. The temperature is usually too hot in dehydrators that just have an on/off switch.
- Rather than buying a dehydrator with a built-in timer, get an inexpensive timer from a hardware store—the kind they sell for Christmas lights and security lighting.
- To make crackers or foods that start out a bit runny, you'll need special sheets. Excalibur's sheets are called "teflex" (because they contain teflon). They are very durable and easy to use. The plastic sheets that come with round dehydrators are usually very thick and have curved edges, so I find it harder to make crackers with them. Lately I've been using parchment paper instead of teflex or plastic. Some air flows through parchment, so food dehydrates a bit faster than using teflex or plastic. Note that if left too long, parchment is hard to remove because food starts to adhere to it.

- LEMON JUICER – There are lots of different kinds of lemon juicers, both manual and electric. I found a manual metal one that I love. You put half a lemon in the hollow of one side, then bring the other side down to press out the juice. The seeds usually stay in the lemon. Another juicer that gets lots of juice out is a reamer, which is made of wood. Press and twist the reamer inside half a lemon to get the juice out, then strain the lemon juice to remove the seeds, or just pick the seeds out with a spoon.

- GARLIC PRESS – Years ago I finely chopped garlic using a knife. Now I wouldn't be without a garlic press because it makes it so quick and easy, plus it cuts garlic finer than I can with a knife.

- SPATULAS – For scraping the insides of the blender and food processor.

- JULIENNE PEELER – This is a great device for making Pasta (see Spaghetti / Pasta recipe). Sometimes I use a julienne peeler, instead of a grater, to cut carrots for salad or to use as a garnish.

- SPROUTING JARS – See information on Sprouting (page 37).

- NUT MYLK / SPROUTING BAG – See information under Nut Mylk and under Sprouting for uses of this cloth mesh bag with a drawstring. A large metal strainer will also strain NutMylk, but the bag is easier to use.

- MEASURING CUPS AND SPOONS – To try lots of recipes.

- ICE CREAM SCOOPER – A spring-loaded scooper makes it easier to measure Pizza Crusts, Neatballs, Sunburgers and Veggie Bites on parchment, teflex or plastic sheets for dehydrating.

FOOD STAPLES:
I store most foods, including spices, in the fridge so that they stay as fresh as possible. I prefer to store food in glass jars rather than in plastic. It's also nice to have some herbs, like rosemary or thyme, growing in pots or in an herb garden. Here are foods I normally have in my kitchen. I was surprised to see how long the list is. Remember that these are the things I like to have around, but your list may look different. I've included everything to give you ideas.

Food Staples I Don't Refrigerate:
- agave nectar (raw)
- apple cider vinegar (unpasteurized)
- crackers I've made stored in metal cookie tins or glass jars
- fruit that is ripening (e.g. bananas, pears, avocados, tomatoes)
- garlic (my recipes are based on garlic cloves of average strength)
- nori sheets (dried, not roasted or toasted – truly raw nori sheets aren't green; they are dark purple/black)

- olive oil
- red or white onions
- sea salt (I use a wonderful brand called Nature's Cargo)

Refrigerated Food Staples:
- almonds
- beets
- carob powder and cacao powder (both raw)
- carrots
- celery
- dates (including dates soaking in water to use for sweetener or in recipes)
- dulse (I use whole dulse, rather than dulse flakes)
- flax seeds (brown, but sometimes I also have golden flax seeds)
- fruit, including avocados and other fruits that don't need to be ripened yet (e.g. apples, pears, seasonal fruits)
- green onions
- greens (vary the greens you use – see Smoothies section for ideas)
- hemp seeds
- lemons and limes (an average lemon yields 2 tablespoons juice)
- parsley (I prefer Italian parsley, but curly is good too)
- pecans (I use pecans instead of walnuts because walnuts are often rancid.)
- pumpkin seeds
- quinoa
- raisins (I prefer Sultana because they have seeds; therefore they are less hybridized. Also, other raisins are often coated with oil.)
- seeds for sprouting (I like alfalfa, red clover and fenugreek)
- sesame seeds (unhulled)
- steel cut oats
- sun dried tomatoes (dry, not yet hydrated in water or oil)
- sunflower seeds (hulled)
- tahini (raw – from ground sesame seeds)

Spices:
I store spices in the fridge in small glass spice jars, with the month and year of purchase written on a label. Sometimes I try different spices for variety and for the beneficial properties they may have. Here are the spices I normally have in my fridge:
- allspice
- caraway seeds
- cardamom
- cayenne
- celery seeds
- chili powder
- cinnamon
- cloves (whole and ground)
- cumin (whole and ground)
- curry powder
- ginger root (fresh)
- Italian spices (a packaged combination which may contain basil, oregano, rosemary, savory and sage)
- nutmeg (ground)
- paprika
- poppy seeds
- poultry spice (a packaged combination which usually contains sage, rosemary, thyme, savory and marjoram)
- turmeric

Other Foods I Sometimes Have:
- Brazil nuts, macadamia nuts and pine nuts
- cilantro (fresh)
- cucumbers
- dill (fresh)
- durian (a sensuous fruit from Asian stores – normally sold frozen)
- fruits, vegetables and herbs that are in season
- goji berries (dried)
- mushrooms
- radishes (red or daikon)
- red, orange or yellow peppers

IS IT RAW?

I was first inspired to write this book because I wanted to provide recipes that contain only raw ingredients. To make the transition to a raw diet easier, most raw books include some foods that aren't raw. I've found many people, including myself, assumed these foods were raw because they were in the books. Here's some information to let you know what's raw and what isn't.

ALCOHOL – Red wine is the only raw alcohol I'm aware of. Note that red wine may contain sulphates.

ALMONDS – Since September 2007, most almonds grown in California are pasteurized. Various methods are used - gas, steam, irradiation. Organic almonds are steamed for just a few seconds, so that they are still viable; therefore they are raw. I recommend that you buy organic almonds. If they sprout when you soak them, you'll know they are raw.

CASHEWS – 'Raw' cashews are labeled 'raw' because they're not roasted. Actually they aren't raw because the cashew shell is steamed at high temperatures to remove the nut from the shell, thus cooking the nut inside. A toxic resin inside the shell will make the nut inedible if the shell isn't opened properly. Suppliers of truly raw cashews use specially designed tools to split open each cashew shell by hand. There are a number of suppliers of truly raw cashews such as Navitas Naturals, www.realrawfoods.com and www.rawfood.com.

DATES – Dates sold as "pitted dates" are normally steamed in order to remove the pits; therefore they aren't raw. There are a number of different kinds of whole dates available (e.g. medjool, halawi, kadrawi and deglet noor).

DEHYDRATED FOODS – I usually start dehydrating at 120 degrees Fahrenheit (48.7 Celsius) for the first hour, then turn down to 105 degrees Fahrenheit (40.6 Celsius) for the remainder of the time (the moisture in food keeps the temperature below 105 degrees in the first hour). Dehydrating food destroys some of the enzymes, although the food will still have more life than cooked foods. Higher temperatures destroy the enzymes. Note that there are various opinions about the appropriate temperature to use, with some raw fooders using temperatures higher than 105 degrees, such as 118 degrees. Drying time is affected by the humidity in the kitchen and other foods in the dehydrator. If dehydrating several recipes at the same time, note that strong smelling recipes (e.g. containing cumin, curry, garlic, or onion) may affect the flavour of other recipes (e.g. cookies or Fruit Rollups).

DRIED FRUITS – Most dried fruits sold in stores are dried at high temperatures and often have sulphites and/or sugar added. Banana chips are normally made from unripe banana or plantain slices, with sulphites added before they are fried in oil. Sun-dried fruits are raw.
Although it's best to eat fresh fruits, dried fruits come in handy for traveling and for a treat. You can dehydrate your own fruits. See the recipe for Dehydrated Bananas.

FROZEN FOODS – Nuts and seeds freeze in Northern climates in the winter—they still sprout. Therefore it's fine to store raw nuts and seeds in the freezer. Vegetables and some fruits are usually blanched before freezing in order to kill enzymes that cause deterioration of the food; therefore blanched foods aren't raw. Some fruits, such as berries, bananas, peaches, plums, nectarines, apricots and tomatoes, can be frozen and are still raw, although there is a loss of enzymes.

HONEY – Unless labeled as unpasteurized, most honey isn't raw because it's heated at a high temperature. Unpasteurized honey is a raw food, but isn't a vegan food because it's an animal product. Some raw fooders use unpasteurized honey. My recipes use sweeteners such as raw agave nectar, raisins, dates, prunes, apricots or water from soaking dates.

JUICE - Bottled or frozen concentrated juice has been pasteurized in order to have a long shelf life. Only freshly made juice is raw.

MAPLE SYRUP - Forty cups of sap is boiled to produce one cup of maple syrup; therefore maple syrup isn't raw.

NORI – Nori is a sea vegetable purchased in packages of 6"x8" sheets for making Nori Rolls and Nori Snacks (see recipes). If the package says 'toasted' or 'roasted', then it isn't raw. Raw Nori is dark purple or black, rather than green and may be labeled 'dried'.

NUTS – Most nuts are available roasted, blanched or raw. If they have a coating, are salted, roasted or blanched, they aren't raw. Note that white nuts such as Brazil and macadamias are rancid if they have a yellowish colour. See page 31 regarding cashews.

NUTRITIONAL YEAST – Yeast is grown on mineral enriched molasses. At the end of the growth period, the culture is pasteurized to kill the yeast. This isn't a raw or living food.

OATS – Rolled oats are steamed before rolling them; therefore they aren't raw. Steel cut oats and Scottish oats are raw.

OILS – Most oils are heated in processing so they don't go rancid quickly. They're usually labeled 'refined'. Look for unrefined, cold-pressed or stone-pressed extra virgin oils. Ideally use an avocado, olives, hemp seeds, or a coconut instead of oil.

OLIVES – Most canned olives are cooked in the canning process, so they aren't raw. Look for olives sold in serve-yourself bulk bins. My favourite olives are sun dried, or kalamata. Most olives are preserved with salt, so it's good to rinse and soak them in water.

SALT – Many salts sold are baked, bleached and/or have added sugar, iodine, etc. Celtic sea salt or other sun-dried salts are raw, but should be used sparingly. Celery and sea vegetables contain natural salts.

SOY PRODUCTS (Miso, Nama Shoyu, Tamari, Braggs Amino Acids) – I don't eat Miso or Nama Shoya because they're started using cooked soybeans and are salty. However, they are living foods and some raw fooders consider them to be an important addition to their diet.

- Miso is made from cooked soybeans which have been inoculated with bacteria and fermented for up to three years. It's sometimes mixed with various grains. Unpasteurized miso is a condiment which can be added to savoury dishes where you might otherwise use salt.

- Nama Shoyu, organic and unpasteurized, by Ohsawa, is the only 'live' soy sauce on the market at this time.

- Tamari is pasteurized, so it isn't raw or living.

- Braggs isn't raw or living. Although Braggs won't reveal the process, some experts believe it's processed with heat and hydrochloric acid. Salt forms in processing, plus glutamic acid, which is in MSG.

SPICES – Many spices are dried at high temperatures and/or irradiated. Get spices from a good source or grow your own.

VANILLA EXTRACT – It isn't raw because vanilla beans are soaked in ethyl alcohol and water. Sometimes heat is added to create the best extraction. For vanilla flavour use vanilla beans.

VINEGAR – Apple cider vinegar seems to be the only unpasteurized vinegar available. There's some disagreement as to whether unpasteurized apple cider is acidic, or alkaline-forming in the body. Some people swear by it as a tonic; whereas others believe it should be avoided because it's acidic. I limit its use, preferring lemon juice in most salads.

WILD RICE – This is actually a grass seed, not rice and isn't raw. Seeds are processed at over 200 degrees to remove the husks and to kill bacteria. I confirmed this with the Canadian Wild Rice Council because I used to love eating wild rice.

MORE RAW NIT-PICKING

Here's some additional info about raw foods:

SESAME SEEDS - For years I was using hulled sesame seeds because oxalic acid on unhulled sesame seeds inhibits calcium utilization, and unhulled sesame seeds can taste bitter. Recently I learned that hulled sesame seeds won't sprout, which means they aren't raw. Also, hulled sesame seeds are often treated with chemicals to soften the hull. As a result, I now use unhulled sesame seeds, usually soaking the unhulled seeds for a few minutes, or just rinsing them in a strainer.

SOAKING NUTS AND SEEDS – Nuts and seeds contain enzyme inhibitors which preserve them from sprouting until conditions are right for them to grow (warm, moist soil). If enzyme inhibitors aren't removed, nuts and seeds increase the acidity in our system and may inhibit the breakdown of nutrients. Ideally nuts and seeds should be soaked, then drained and rinsed before using. Besides removing enzyme inhibitors, soaking starts the sprouting process which gives us more nutrients. Approximate soaking times are:

- eight to twelve hours for almonds
- four to eight hours for hazelnuts, pecans, pumpkin seeds, sunflower seeds and walnuts
- up to two hours, or just a rinse for sesame seeds
- no soaking required for cashews, flax seeds, hemp, macadamia nuts or pinenuts.

FERMENTED FOODS – It's beneficial to eat fermented foods, especially if you have ever taken antibiotics. They provide our body with probiotics (good bacteria) and B complex vitamins. Fermenting Veggie Pates breaks down the dense fibers of nuts and seeds, making them more digestible. You can make your own Sauerkraut, or buy refrigerated, unpasteurized Sauerkraut in your health food store.

FLAX SEEDS AND PSYLLIUM HUSKS AS BINDERS - Flax seeds become gelatinous when they get wet; so they act like a glue in recipes. Due to their flavour, they are best in savoury recipes. For sweet recipes use a little, or use ground sesame seeds to absorb some of the moisture. Ground psyllium husks can also be used as a binder, but don't use too much because the taste of psyllium may become noticeable.

FOOD COMBINING

Some foods take longer to digest than others. The digestion times of raw foods are:

Very Fast – melon, fruit, juices, smoothies without fat
Fast   – greens, vegetables, smoothies with fat
Slow   – grains, avocado, oil, nuts, seeds, dehydrated foods

When we eat foods that have slow digestion times and follow them with a food that is very fast, the very fast food may stay in the stomach for too long and ferment.

Often fruits are served as a dessert, but this isn't proper food combining and can result in gas and bloating. Fruits are best eaten on their own, although greens combine well with any food. We usually feel better eating melons before other fruits.

Most raw pies are made of nuts and fruits, which have different digestion rates. They are usually processed using a food processor or blender, which lessens the impact of poor food combining. The occasional combination of fruits and fats is okay, but avoiding excessive eating of these combinations will help your digestion.

It's good to know about proper food combining, but listen to what your body is telling you.

SPROUTING

Almost any seed, grain or legume can be sprouted. Most seeds yield six to ten times their weight in sprouts. During the sprouting process vitamins, minerals, proteins and enzymes are produced at an incredible rate. When camping or traveling, you can use a sprouting bag or jar to enjoy the benefits of growing your own sprouts.

Large seeds sprout easily in a sprouting bag or in a jar:
adzuki beans, almonds, barley, buckwheat (unhulled), chickpeas, corn, fenugreek, kidney beans, lentils, millet, mung beans, oats, peas, pinto beans, pumpkin, rye, spelt, sunflower (unhulled), wheat

Small seeds are best sprouted in a jar because their tiny shoots latch onto the material of a sprouting bag. Leave them in direct light the day before harvest for optimum chlorophyll development:
alfalfa, broccoli, cabbage, clover, mustard, quinoa, radish, spinach

SPROUTING PROCESS:

SOAK - Put small or large seeds in a jar, add water to at least three times the level of seeds, cover with a screen and secure with a rubber band. Large seeds can be poured into a sprout bag instead of a jar; immerse the bag in a bowl of water. Allow small seeds to soak four to six hours, grains and larger seeds eight to twelve hours.

DRAIN - Drain the soak water and rinse with fresh water. If using a bag, hang the bag on a hook to drain, with a bowl (or plastic bag if you're traveling) under the bag. If using a jar, place the jar in a bowl, tilting the jar downward at a 45 degree angle, so air can get in.

RINSE - Using cool water, rinse and drain twice a day to ensure sprouts are moist without getting mouldy.

HARVEST – Sprout times vary from one to six days, depending on what is being sprouted and whether it gets green. To remove the outer layer (hulls) of small seeds, fill the jar with water. Hulls will rise to the surface and can be scooped off. Note that buckwheat and sunflower seeds need to be planted in soil to obtain green sprouts.

MENU PLANNING

Raw food preparation isn't complicated, but it may take time for 'uncooking' to be natural for you. Remember that you weren't born with the know-how to cook—you had years to learn. Raw food preparation is just another way of preparing food. As time goes on you'll even find 'uncooking' easier than cooking. Cleanup is easier too because you won't be scrubbing baked-on food from pots and pans.

One thing that helps is to make a weekly menu plan, or at least make a menu plan for a special event. You may need to soak and sprout seeds for a recipe which also requires dehydrating. You might want to add extra seeds to sprout for use in another meal. By planning in advance, your selection of tasty recipes won't be limited to foods that don't require soaking, sprouting and/or dehydrating.

Consider whether some items can be made hours, or even days, before the event so that you aren't doing everything at the last minute. For example, if you want to serve Pizza:
- Pizza Crusts can be made several weeks ahead of time.
- Barbeque Sauce and Marinated Mushrooms can be made days ahead.
- Sunny Spread can be made a day or two ahead.
- Olives and peppers can be sliced several hours before assembling the Pizza.

To ensure avocados don't have bruises, buy them when they're hard and the skin is a lime green colour. Store in the fridge until two days before you need to use (three days if the room temperature is cool), then put them in a basket so they won't be handled until they're ripe.

THE FIVE TASTES

You will make delicious raw food if you have all five of these tastes in your recipes. Here are some examples:

SWEET	SOUR	SALTY	SPICY	BITTER
banana	lemon	sea salt	cayenne	kale
dates	lime	celery	hot pepper	lettuce
apples	apple cider	dulse	garlic	herbs
mangos	vinegar	kelp	onion	spices
papaya	orange	nori	ginger	parsley
raisins	grapefruit	arame	mustard seeds	arugala
red pepper	rhubarb		radish	celery tops
carrots	sorrel		horseradish	dandelion
beets	tomato		wasabi	
tomato	nut yogyrt		cinnamon	

The ratios will change with each dish. The key to creating great raw recipes is to balance the five tastes. When you are done preparing a dish, be sure to taste it, asking yourself whether it needs more of any of the tastes. Note the following:

- Excess SOUR is balanced by adding SWEET.

- Overly BITTER is balanced by adding SOUR.

- FATS tone down SPICES and mellow too much SWEETNESS.

- SALT brings out flavours. It is the most concentrated, so use little.

- BITTER accents the SWEET. Use carefully so the BITTER isn't overpowering.

FOODS FOR INTERNATIONAL FLAVOURS

Here are some foods to help you achieve a taste you're looking for, or to give you some ideas:

Chinese: licorice, ginger, vinegar, garlic, fennel, cinnamon, cloves

Indian: cumin, coriander, cinnamon, nutmeg, curry, turmeric, garam masala, ginger, cloves

Italian: basil, parsley, oregano, rosemary, thyme, garlic

Mexican: cumin, coriander, cilantro, chili powder, hot peppers, garlic, lime

Russian: dill, parsley, scallion, garlic, coriander, caraway

Thai: cilantro, lemongrass, cumin, curry, ginger, coconut

PHOTOGRAPHS

- Amazing Avocados on sprouts (page 83)
- Salad Ideas (page 107)
- Savoury Crackers (page 110)
- Marinara Sauce (page 75)
- Apple Pie (page 128)

- Neatloaf (page 95)

• Tomato Salad (page 120)

• Beet Soup (page 70)

• Oriental Salad (page 101)

· Truffles (page 152)

· Truffle Fruit Pie (page 151)

· Chocolate Brownies (page 135)

· Seasoned Nuts & Seeds using
  Cinnamon & Nutmeg (page 112)

· Chai Nut Mylk (page 51)

· Strawberry Smoothie (page 64)
· Green Smoothie (page 60)

· Orange Sesame Chewies (page 147)

· Pizza (page 104):
  · Marinated Mushrooms (page 94)
  · Barbeque Sauce (page 69)
  · red & yellow peppers
  · olives
  · basil
  · Pizza Crusts (page 103)

· Carrot Cake & Icing (page 134)

- Sunburgers (page 116)
- Chili Sauce (page 72)
- Better than Mayo (page 71)
- romaine lettuce, tomatoes, cucumbers, dill and red onion

- Tortilla Chips (page 121)

- Oatmeal with banana and blueberries on top (page 52)

- Veggie Pate in peppers and in a bowl (page 124)
- Savoury Crackers (page 110)

- Nori Rolls (page 97)   · Pickled Ginger - both kinds (page 102)
- Sweet & Sour Sauce served in half a scooped out lime (page 80)

• Banana Lemon Pie with poppy seeds and raspberries (page 131)

• Lisa's Raw Dinner Plate

CHAPTER 3 - BEVERAGES & OTHER BREAKFAST ITEMS

For many years I've enjoyed the energy and mental clarity that fruit provides. Having only fruit in the morning increases mental clarity because our digestive system doesn't use a lot of energy to digest the food. Fruit also helps with better elimination. On days when I need to concentrate more, I continue eating fruit or Smoothies.

Remember that breakfast (or any meal) can be as simple as eating some fruit or having a Smoothie. Fruit salads can be luscious.

AVOCADO & MANGO

This tasty combination is perfect for breakfast, lunch, supper or for a snack!

Extra Prep Time: None
Quantity: approximately 1 cup

Ingredients:
- 1 avocado
- 1 mango
- 1 dash of sea salt (optional)

⇒ Cut avocado and mango in 1" chunks and put in a serving bowl. Add a dash of salt to enhance the flavours.

NUT MYLKS AND YOGYRT

Nut Mylks are tasty and nutritious alternatives to dairy. Drink the Mylk or pour it on cereal. It's a great base for smoothies, soups and salad dressings. Fermenting Mylk to make Yogyrt makes it even more digestible.

Add the pulp to cereals or cookie dough (see Apple Carrot Cookies recipe), use as a base for salads (see Seedy Salad recipe) or Veggie Pate (see Veggie Pate recipe).

Extra Prep Time: Soak nuts and seeds for four to twelve hours (two hours for sesame seeds)

Quantity: 2 1/2 cups of Nut Mylk, and 1 cup of nut pulp

Ingredients:
- 1 cup dry unhulled sesame seeds (rich in calcium and magnesium),
 OR 1/2 cup dry almonds (rich in calcium),
 OR 3/4 cup dry sunflower seeds (high in protein),
 OR 3/4 cup dry pumpkin seeds (high in zinc),
 OR a combination of nuts and seeds.
- 2 1/2 cups water (for blending)
- 1/3 cup raisins, dates, dried apricots, dried figs, or prunes
- pinch of sea salt

⇒ Soak sesame seeds for two hours; hazelnuts, pecans, pumpkin seeds, sunflower seeds and walnuts for four to eight hours; almonds for eight to twelve hours. Discard soaking water and rinse.

⇒ For a smoother texture when using sesame seeds, especially if you don't have a powerful blender, grind unsoaked sesame seeds in a coffee grinder before blending. Blend all ingredients. Strain through a nut mylk bag or a metal strainer.

CONTINUED ON NEXT PAGE

NUTMYLKS & YOGYRT CONTINUED:

<u>Variations:</u>

Pour strained Mylk back in the blender to blend in some or all of the following:

- 1 or 2 bananas - makes the Mylk very creamy and sweet
- cinnamon, or carob powder
- blueberries, strawberries or raspberries

- To make <u>Chai Nut Mylk</u> (exceptionally tasty using almond mylk and a banana), add the following to 2 1/2 cups strained Nut Mylk:

- 1 teaspoon chopped ginger
- 1/2 teaspoon cardamom
- 1/2 teaspoon cinnamon
- 1/4 teaspoon carob powder
- pinches of nutmeg and allspice

- To make <u>Yogyrt</u>, pour Nut Mylk in a container and cover with a cloth. Leave undisturbed on the counter (or in the fridge to separate without fermenting) for about ten hours, so it can thicken and separate like curds and whey. Refrigerate. The thick part is Yogyrt. Note that it's not as thick as yogurt made from dairy milk. You can drink the thin part or use as a base in a soup or salad dressing.

OATMEAL

A bowl of Oatmeal in the morning (or anytime) is tasty and will keep you satisfied for several hours.

Extra Prep Time: Can be made without presoaking, but consistency is smoother if soaked for eight to twelve hours.

Quantity: 1 1/2 cups (for one hungry person)

Ingredients:
- 1/2 cup steel-cut oats
- 1 1/2 tablespoons raisins
- 1 teaspoon cinnamon, plus a sprinkle as a garnish when serving
- 3/4 cup water
- apple or pear, chopped but not peeled or cored
- banana and/or berries, fruit slices such as peach, nectarine, plum (optional)

⇒ Soak oats, raisins and cinnamon in the water for eight to twelve hours in a covered bowl (or in the blender) left on the counter.

⇒ Blend the soaked ingredients and the apple or pear.

⇒ Serve in a bowl. Sprinkle with a bit of cinnamon. Yummy with banana slices, berries and/or fruit slices on top. Oatmeal is also nice with a bit of Nut Mylk poured over it (see Nut Mylk recipe).

REJUVELAC

Rejuvelac is tasty, has many health benefits and is easy to make. It contains B complex Vitamins and is rich in Vitamin B12. Rejuvelac contains friendly bacteria and lots of enzymes. The proteins and starches contained in Rejuvelac are broken down to their simplest forms...amino acids and simple sugars...making the nutrients immediately available for assimilation, even for people with weak digestive systems. Using Rejuvelac in recipes, instead of water, helps preserve the ingredients because Rejuvelac's vitamin E content acts as an antioxidant. Rejuvelac is normally made with wheat berries, which are wheat seeds for growing wheat, or wheatgrass. People with wheat sensitivities do not have problems, but some use rye instead of wheat berries.

You may see recipes for the "whole berry method" of making Rejuvelac (wheat berries are not ground up). The recipe below makes a tarter, more flavourful Rejuvelac than the whole berry method. Also, fermentation is more complete because more of the seed is exposed to water, resulting in Rejuvelac that is nutritionally superior.

Extra Prep Time: - Soak wheat berries for ten to twelve hours.
- Sprout for 24 hours.
- After blending, let stand for two to four days.

Quantity: 14 cups

Ingredients:
- 1/3 cup soft wheat berries (= approximately 1 cup sprouted)
- 15 cups water (Tap water is OK to use because the fermentation process cleans it.)

⇒ Soak wheat berries ten to twelve hours. Drain and rinse.

⇒ Rinsing twice a day, let wheat berries sprout for at least 24 hours... until there are white tails no longer than the length of the berries. If you don't have time to proceed immediately, refrigerate to slow sprouting.

CONTINUED ON NEXT PAGE

REJUVELAC CONTINUED:

⇒ Blend sprouted seeds and some water in a blender. Pour into a one gallon glass jar and fill with water. Cover the opening with a cloth.

⇒ Let jar stand at room temperature for two to four days, stirring VERY gently twice a day with a wooden spoon (Don't use metal.) Fermentation occurs more quickly when the room temperature is high. On a hot day, Rejuvelac may be ready in as little as one day. It's ready when it has a fermented smell and tastes somewhat like unsweetened lemonade. Using cheesecloth, or a strainer, pour the liquid into a glass jar for drinking and discard the wheat berries. If Rejuvelac has a foul smell, bad bacteria has affected it, so it should be discarded. Rejuvelac will keep four to seven days, if refrigerated.

SIMPLY H2O + LEMON

You can't get much easier than this, unless you serve plain water! Slices of lemon not only give the water a bit of flavour and help make your body more alkaline--they also make the drink look attractive.

If you are going hiking for the day, add a slice or two of lemon to your water bottle to make the water more refreshing. Of course you don't need to go on a hike to enjoy a slice of lemon in a glass of water.

Extra Prep Time: None
Quantity: 8 cups

Ingredients:
- 8 cups water
- 1/2 lemon (1/4"-1/2" thick slices, unpeeled, seeds removed)

⇒ Pour water into a glass pitcher.

⇒ Add the lemon slices to the water. Can be left out at room temperature for several hours, or placed in the fridge. It will keep well for a few days if refrigerated.

SMOOTHIES

Smoothies are a quick and easy way to enjoy raw foods. Just chop and blend the ingredients, then drink. Leftovers can be dehydrated to make tasty Fruit Roll-Ups (see recipe). When Smoothies are blended well, their nutrients are easily absorbed and our bodies don't use a lot of energy digesting the Smoothie.

Liquids and soft foods go in the blender first, then hard items and ice. Cut food into 1" to 3" pieces, with hard ingredients as small as practical. Solid frozen fruit is extremely hard to blend, so let it partially thaw before blending. Allow enough liquid or juicy fruits to ease the blending process. Smoothies taste best and are most nutritious fresh from the blender. To preserve freshness for several hours away from home, add ice to the Smoothie after blending.

I highly recommend Victoria Boutenko's book *Green For Life*, which talks about the advantages of drinking Green Smoothies. If your Smoothie consists of approximately 60% fruit and 40% greens, it won't taste "green" and will provide you with minerals and vitamins your body needs. When using greens that are strong-flavoured or when using a lot of greens, adding lemon makes the Smoothie more palatable. Most people love the taste and texture of Green Smoothies right away. You may want to start by adding only one or two leaves of a mild green leafy vegetable, such as romaine lettuce, to your fruit smoothie.

Include any of the following items in a Smoothie:

LIQUID:
- water and/or ice cubes (small ice cubes are easier on your blender)
- fresh apple, orange, grapefruit or carrot juice

FOR BODY (plus flavour, minerals and vitamins):
- apple (unpeeled)
- apricot (fresh or dried, unsulphured)

CONTINUED ON NEXT PAGE

SMOOTHIES CONTINUED:

- banana (fresh or frozen) – adds sweetness and smooth texture
- berries (fresh or frozen blackberries, blueberries, cranberries, raspberries, strawberries)
- coconut (meat and juice)
- cucumber
- currants
- dates - adds concentrated sweetness
- figs
- grapefruit (remove and discard the peel)
- grapes or raisins
- lemons (if organic: remove some or all of the peel, if not organic: remove peel. Lemons make greens more palatable and our body alkaline)
- lime (remove the peel)
- mangos (peeled and seed removed)
- oranges (peeled)
- papayas (peeled and most of seeds removed)
- peaches or nectarines (unpeeled and stone removed)
- pears (unpeeled)
- pineapples (cut off outer skin and leaves)
- plums or prunes (stone removed)
- watermelon or other melons (remove outer skin; include some of the green portion of watermelon if its organic)

FOR EXTRA PROTEIN, MINERALS, OR A DIFFERENT TEXTURE:
- almonds (soaked – alkalizing and rich in calcium)
- goji berries (dried)
- greens (beet greens, carrot tops, celery, chard, dandelion greens, edible weeds such as stinging nettles or chickweed, fennel, grape leaves, kale, lettuces such as romaine, green or red leaf, mint, mixed greens, parsley, spinach, sprouts)
- flax seeds (ground – high in nutrients and essential fatty acids)
- hemp seeds (unsoaked – high in complete protein, essential fatty acids)

CONTINUED ON NEXT PAGE

SMOOTHIES CONTINUED:

- pumpkin seeds (soaked – high in zinc)
- sesame seeds (unhulled, best if rinsed or soaked a few hours—rich in calcium and magnesium. If not rinsed or soaked, sesame seeds can be ground in a coffee grinder for a smoother texture.)
- sunflower seeds (soaked – high in complete protein)

FOR A CREAMY TEXTURE:
- avocado (Always blend as the last item. Do not over blend.)
- bananas (add sweetness and smooth texture)

FOR EXTRA SWEETNESS:
- more fruit, especially banana
- a few dates or raisins
- a very small amount of dried stevia leaves (a little goes a long way!)

FOR ADDITIONAL FLAVOUR (Note: bitter brings out sweetness):
- allspice
- cinnamon
- cloves
- ginger (fresh)
- lemon rind (grated)
- nutmeg

CREAMSICLE SMOOTHIE

Mmmm......you'll love the yummy taste. The creamy texture will make you think you're eating a cloud.

Extra Prep Time: None
Quantity: 2 1/2 cups

Ingredients:
- 1/2 cup water
- 1 cup cantelope (peeled and seeds removed)
- 1 orange (peeled)
- 1 banana

⇒ Blend all ingredients until smooth.

GREEN SMOOTHIE

This is the Smoothie I usually make for breakfast. Note that I use many different variations of fruit, spices and greens, etc. so each day I enjoy a different smoothie. Please refer to previous pages for more information on Smoothies.

Extra Prep Time: None
Quantity: 4 to 5 cups

Ingredients:
- 1 1/2 cups water
- 1 pear (or apple, peach, mango, 2 nectarines, 2 plums, 2 apricots, 1/2 cup grapes, 1-2 stalks rhubarb)
- 1/2 cup berries (raspberries, blueberries, blackberries or strawberries)
- 1 banana
- 1/2 - 1 lemon (if organic, include one tablespoon of peel)
- 1 teaspoon fresh ginger (or 1/8 teaspoon cinnamon, nutmeg, allspice or a clove)
- 1 1/2 packed cups greens (e.g. kale, romaine, spinach, parsley, chard, beet greens, some dandelion greens or other bitter greens, mixed greens, carrot tops, or edible weeds)
- 1/4 cup dates (optional – for a sweeter Smoothie)
- 1 tablespoon hemp seeds or sesame seeds (optional)

⇒ Blend all ingredients until smooth.

LEMONADE SMOOTHIE

Besides having a refreshing taste, Lemonade Smoothies help make your body more alkaline (which is a good thing ☺).

Extra Prep Time: None
Quantity: 2 cups

Ingredients:
- 1 cup water
- 1 lemon (peeled – include 1 tablespoon of peel if the lemon is organic)
- 1 banana
- 1/3 cup dates (measure after removing pits)
- 1/2 stalk celery, including leaves

⇒ Blend all ingredients until smooth.

ORANGE BANANA GREEN SMOOTHIE

Get your citrus fix with this tasty smoothie!

Extra Prep Time: None
Quantity: 4 cups

Ingredients:
- 1 1/2 cups water
- 2 oranges (peeled)
- 1 banana
- 1/2 teaspoon fresh ginger
- 1/4 cup dates (measuring after removing pits)
- 1 stalk celery
- 1/2 cup mild tasting greens (e.g. carrot tops, parsley, kale)
- 1 tablespoon hemp nuts, or sesame seeds (optional)

⇒ Blend all ingredients until smooth.

PEACH SMOOTHIE

Cucumber or romaine keep this Smoothie light, and allow the peach or nectarine flavour to come out. Lemon provides a hint of tartness.

Extra Prep Time: None
Quantity: 5 1/2 cups

Ingredients:
- 1 1/2 cups water
- 3 peaches, or nectarines (unpeeled)
- 1 banana
- 1/2 lemon (peeled)
- 1 1/2 cups cucumber, or 1 1/2 cups romaine lettuce
- 1/8 teaspoon allspice (optional)

⇒ Blend all ingredients until smooth.

STRAWBERRY SMOOTHIE

The scrumptious strawberry taste stands out in this smoothie.

Extra Prep Time: None
Quantity: 2 cups

Ingredients:
- 1 cup water
- 5 strawberries (include leaves if they are fresh)
- 1 banana
- 1 stalk celery
- dash of allspice (or cinnamon, clove, ginger or nutmeg)

⇒ Blend all ingredients until smooth.

ALTERNATIVES:

- Add lettuce leaf or other greens.

- Add 1 tablespoon hemp seeds, or sesame seeds.

- Add 1 1/2 tablespoons dates.

WATERMELON SMOOTHIE

This is one of my favourite Smoothies. It's very cleansing, hydrating, energizing, easy to prepare and tastes so good!

Extra Prep Time: None
Quantity: as much as you decide to make – Sometimes I drink a quarter or half a watermelon as my breakfast and lunch.

Ingredients:
- watermelon

⇒ Discard the green skin. You might include a bit of the skin if the watermelon is organic; however it usually doesn't blend thoroughly. Cut the red and white parts into 2"- 4" pieces. Put the juicy middle portion of the watermelon in the bottom of the blender to make it easier to blend. Blend until smooth. The pulp will gradually float to the surface of your glass, so keep a spoon handy to stir the pulp back into the liquid.

TEA - SUN TEA / GINGER TEA

<u>SUN TEA</u>: Besides having a wonderful flavour, Sun Tea is refreshing and easy to make. Spearmint and peppermint are the most popular mints. Mint is a perennial plant which is easy to grow in full sun with lots of water. Therefore, besides enjoying mint bought at the store, you can prepare tea fresh from your garden.

Extra Prep Time: Soak for 12 to 24 hours to bring out the flavour.
Quantity: 8 cups

Ingredients:
- 1 cup fresh mint leaves
- 8 cups water

⇒ Place mint in a glass pitcher or jar. Add water. Cover with a lid or cloth and place on the counter or in the sun for 12 to 24 hours so the mint flavour can go into the water.

⇒ When it's ready to drink, Sun Tea can be left out at room temperature for several hours, or placed in the fridge. It will keep well for a few days if refrigerated.

<u>GINGER TEA</u>: Ginger Tea is another tasty and soothing tea. Drink it warm or cold.

Extra Prep Time: Steep for 5 minutes or more
Quantity: 1 1/2 cups

Ingredients:
- 1 tablespoon fresh ginger (sliced, but not peeled)
- 1 1/2 cups water (hot, but not boiling)

⇒ Put ginger in a teapot. Add water to the teapot, put the lid on and steep for five minutes or more so the flavour can go into the water. It will keep for a few days if refrigerated.

CHAPTER 4 - SOUPS, SALAD DRESSINGS, SAUCES & DIPS

Soups, Salad Dressings, Sauces and Dips are very similar. Leftovers of one can be used as a base for another.

Soups usually have a fat and a vegetable as the foundation of the soup; whereas salad dressings, sauces and dips have a fat and a sour as the primary flavours. Fats produce a creamy texture and make the mixture more satisfying.

Turn a salad dressing recipe into a dip by using less water or juice, and/ or adding nuts or seeds.

Get inspired to create something new using veggies, seasonings and/or seeds you have on hand.

INGREDIENT SUGGESTIONS FOR CREATING SOUPS, SALAD DRESSINGS, SAUCES AND DIPS:

FAT: olive, flax or hemp oil, avocado, nuts, seeds

SOUR: lemon juice, apple cider vinegar, orange juice, lime juice

FOR BODY: bell peppers, cucumber, tomatoes, zucchini, celery, beets

SWEET: dates, raisins, prunes, figs, papaya, strawberries, blueberries, raspberries, mango, apple, banana, apricot, pear, peach, orange juice

SPICY: garlic, onion, ginger, cayenne, hot peppers, curry

SALTY: sea salt, celery, sea vegetables (e.g. dulse and kelp)

BITTER: herbs, spices, greens, celery tops

SOUP TOPPINGS:

Add some of these toppings for texture, flavour and eye appeal:

- herbs such as parsley, dill or basil
- avocado (1/4 to 1/2 inch chunks)
- tomatoes (chopped)
- red, yellow or orange peppers (chopped fine)
- celery (chopped)
- broccoli (chopped fine)
- small pieces of dulse (a sea vegetable)
- pine nuts
- sesame seeds or hemp seeds
- Seasoned Nuts & Seeds (see recipe)

FOODS FOR DIPPING:

When selecting which vegetables to use, try for an assortment of colours, shapes and textures so they are more appetizing. Here are some ideas:

- broccoli
- cauliflower
- cucumbers (sticks or slices)
- mushrooms (slices or whole)
- zucchini (sticks or slices)
- carrots (peeled sticks or slices)
- peppers (long slices or chunks)
- jicama (sticks or slices)
- radish (daikon or red)
- celery (sticks - some with leaves)

ASSEMBLING A GREAT SALAD DRESSING:

⇒ Start with a fat and a sour. For a creamy dressing, add more fat.

⇒ For body, add a non-sweet fruit, or just add a bit of water.

⇒ Add sweet, spicy, salty and bitter foods. The tastes that usually dominate in a good dressing are sour, spicy, then sweet.

⇒ Keep in mind that the salad itself may have some fat (nuts, seeds, avocado), sweetness (raisins), spice (green onion), saltiness (celery, olives, dulse) and bitterness (greens and veggies).

BARBEQUE SAUCE

This sauce is great on Neatloaf, Sunburgers or Pizza, or served with Neatballs or Veggie Bites. It can be prepared well in advance.

Extra Prep Time: None
Quantity: 2 cups

Ingredients:
- 1 green onion
- 1/2 cup raisins
- 1 tablespoon olive oil
- 1 garlic clove
- 1 teaspoon sea salt
- dash of cayenne, or 1/4 teaspoon chopped jalapeno
- 2 teaspoons Italian spice mix
- 1 1/2 cups tomatoes

⇒ In a food processor, process all the ingredients except tomatoes.

⇒ Add tomatoes to mixture in food processor and process slightly, leaving some lumps. Store in fridge. Barbeque Sauce will stay fresh for a week.

BEET SOUP

People are always amazed at Beet Soup's wonderful assortment of flavours and textures.

Quantity: 3 cups

Extra Prep Time: None

Ingredients:
- 1 cup water
- 1 medium size beet (peeled, cut in chunks)
- 1 stalk celery
- 1 tablespoon olive oil
- 1 tablespoon fresh parsley (to blend)
  + 1 teaspoon fresh chopped parsley (for topping)
- 1 teaspoon raisins
- 1 to 2 cloves garlic
- 1/2 of a medium size lemon (peeled)
- dash of cayenne
- 1 teaspoon pine nuts (for topping)
- 1 avocado (cut into 1/2 - 3/4 inch pieces for topping)
- 1 tablespoon dulse pieces (optional topping)

⇒ Blend the following well: water, beet, celery, oil, parsley, raisins, garlic, lemon and cayenne. Pour into serving bowl.

⇒ Sprinkle top of soup with chopped parsley, pine nuts and avocado. Small pieces of dulse can also be put on top for colour, flavour and nutrition.

BETTER THAN MAYO

Better Than Mayo is great spread on crackers or sliced veggies, used as a dip or salad dressing, or as a topping on Sunburgers.

Extra Prep Time: None
Quantity: 1 3/4 cups

Ingredients:
- 1 1/2 cups macadamia nuts or raw cashews (see page 31 - Is It Raw?)
- 3/4 cup water (1/2 to 2/3 cup for very thick)
- 3 tablespoons olive oil
- 2 tablespoons apple cider vinegar
- 1 teaspoon Italian spices
- 1/2 teaspoon sea salt
- dash of cayenne

⇒ Blend all ingredients until smooth. The mixture will thicken within a few minutes. Store in the fridge. It will stay fresh for a week, but is so tasty you'll probably eat it before the end of the week.

CHILI SAUCE

This is a tasty sauce to serve with Neatballs or Veggie Bites, or to put on Sunburgers. Chili Sauce can be prepared well in advance.

Extra Prep Time: None
Quantity: 3 cups

Ingredients:
- 2 green onions
- 1 stalk celery
- 1/2 cup red, yellow or orange peppers
- 1/2 cup raisins
- 1 tablespoon olive oil
- 1 teaspoon apple cider vinegar
- 1 garlic clove
- 2 tablespoons fresh parsley
- 1 teaspoon chili powder
- 1 1/2 cups tomatoes

⇒ In a food processor, process all the ingredients except tomatoes.

⇒ Add tomatoes to mixture in food processor and process slightly, leaving some lumps. Store in fridge. Chili Sauce will stay fresh for a week.

CREAMY SESAME DRESSING/DIP

This is one of my favourite dips for veggies. It's very tasty and has lots of body to stick to the veggies. For the same reason it also makes a great dressing.

Extra Prep Time: None
Quantity: 3 1/2 cups

Ingredients:
- 1 1/2 cups unhulled sesame seeds (can be soaked for a few hours, drained and rinsed; or just rinsed; or just use dry)
- 1 lemon (peeled)
- 1/4 cup olive oil
- 1 1/2 cups water
- 2 cloves garlic
- 1/4 cup raisins
- 1 stalk celery
- 1/2 teaspoon sea salt
- dash of cayenne
- 2 tablespoons dry Italian spices (or your favourite herbs/spices)

⇒ Blend all ingredients. This dressing/dip keeps in the fridge for several days.

GINGER SAUCE/DRESSING/DIP

Ginger Sauce is a very tasty sauce, dressing or dip. It's good with Falafels, in a RawWrap (see Hummus/Falafels/RawWraps), or as a dip for Veggie Bites. I love using the leftover sauce/dip as a salad dressing.

Extra Prep Time: None
Quantity: 1 cup

Ingredients:
- 1/3 cup olive oil
- 2 lemons (peeled)
- 1 1/2 tablespoons fresh ginger
- 2 cloves garlic
- 1 teaspoon raisins, or 1 date
- 1/2 teaspoon sea salt
- 1 tablespoon fresh parsley

⇒ Blend all ingredients. This sauce/dressing/dip keeps in the fridge for a week.

MARINARA SAUCE

Marinara Sauce is a thick and tasty sauce for Spaghetti, Pasta or Pizza (see recipes). Leftover sauce can be used as a base for salad dressing or soup.

Extra Prep Time: Soak sun dried tomatoes and dates for five hours or more so they will process well.

Quantity: 2 cups

Ingredients:
- 1/2 cup (= 30 grams) sun dried tomatoes (preferably unsulphured)
- 1/3 cup dates (measure after removing pits)
- 1/4 cup olive oil
- 1/4 cup water
- 1 teaspoon dry oregano
- 1 teaspoon sea salt
- 1/8 teaspoon cayenne
- 1 cup fresh tomato (approximately 1 medium tomato) cut in 6 pieces
- 3 garlic cloves
- 1 tablespoon lemon juice
- 5 basil leaves

⇒ In a covered jar at room temperature, soak sun dried tomatoes, dates, olive oil, water, oregano, salt and cayenne, for at least five hours, so they will process well. In a food processor, process until sun dried tomatoes and dates are small pieces.

⇒ Add remaining ingredients to sun dried tomatoes/dates in food processor, and process until fresh tomatoes are small pieces. Marinara Sauce will keep for several days, if refrigerated.

PESTO SAUCE/DRESSING/DIP

This sauce is wonderful on Spaghetti and Pasta (see recipe). For extra flavour and texture, add slices of olives and mushrooms to the Spaghetti and Pasta.

Extra Prep Time: None
Quantity: 2 cups

Ingredients:
- 6 to 10 garlic cloves (depends on how much garlic you enjoy)
- 1 packed cup fresh basil
- 1 cup pine nuts (not soaked)
- 1/3 cup olive oil
- 3 tablespoons lemon juice
- 1/2 teaspoon sea salt
- 2 cups spinach
- 1/2 cup water

⇒ Process garlic, basil and pine nuts in a food processor until ground.

⇒ Add the remaining ingredients to mixture in food processor, and process until creamy. If making dressing, or if sauce is thicker than desired, add a bit of water. Lasts for several days in the fridge.

ALTERNATIVE:
Add 6 sundried tomatoes when adding the remaining ingredients to the mixture in the food processor. If the tomatoes are very dry, add them when processing the garlic, basil and pine nuts.

<u>SAVOURY CARROT SOUP</u>

Extra Prep Time: None
Quantity: 4 cups

Ingredients:
- 2 cups water
- 2 cups carrots (cut in 2" chunks)
- 1 celery stalk
- 1 tablespoon fresh parsley (to blend)
  + 1 tablespoon fresh chopped parsley (for topping)
- 2 green onions (set aside 2 tablespoons of the green portion for topping, chopped fine)
- 1 garlic clove
- 1 medium lemon (peeled)
- 1 teaspoon raisins
- 1 teaspoon pine nuts
- 1 tablespoon olive oil
- 3/4 teaspoon sea salt
- 1/2 teaspoon curry powder
- 1/2 teaspoon cumin
- dash of cayenne
- 1/4 cup red pepper (optional - for topping)

⇒ Blend all ingredients, except toppings (1 tablespoon parsley, 2 tablespoons green portion of green onion and red pepper). Pour into a bowl.

⇒ Sprinkle top of soup with chopped parsley, green onion and red pepper.

SAVOURY DRESSING/DIP

Try this dressing or dip when you're in the mood for something savoury.

Extra Prep Time: Soak sunflower seeds for four to eight hours.
Quantity: 3 cups of dressing or 2 1/2 cups of dip

Ingredients:
- 3/4 cup dry sunflower seeds (= approximately 1 1/4 cup soaked)
- 1 cup water (use 1/2 cup water to make a dip)
- 3/4 cup tomato
- 1/3 cup dates (measure after removing pits)
- 4 cloves garlic
- 2 lemons (peeled)
- 2 tablespoons olive oil
- 1 1/2 tablespoons ground cumin
- 1 teaspoon curry
- 1 teaspoon fresh ginger
- 1 teaspoon sea salt

⇒ Soak sunflower seeds for four to eight hours. Drain and rinse.

⇒ Blend all ingredients. This dressing/dip keeps in the fridge for several days.

SQUASH SOUP

Extra Prep Time: None
Quantity: 6 cups

Ingredients:
- 2 cups water
- 1 1/2 cups butternut squash (peeled and cut in 1 1/2" chunks)
- 1 cup tomatoes (to blend)
  + 1/4 cup finely chopped tomato (for topping)
- 1/4 cup sun dried tomatoes
- 4 prunes (pitted)
- 1 stalk celery
- 1/2 cup parsley (to blend) + 1/4 cup parsley (chopped - for topping)
- 1/2 of a medium size lemon (not peeled if organic)
- 1 clove garlic
- 1 green onion
- 1 teaspoon sea salt
- 1/2 teaspoon fresh ginger
- 1/2 teaspoon cinnamon
- 1/4 teaspoon cayenne or jalapeno
- 1 avocado (1/2 to blend + 1/2 cut into 1/2 inch pieces for topping)
- 1/2 cup red pepper (chopped fine for topping)
- 1 tablespoon pine nuts

⇒ In a blender, blend the following well: water, squash, tomatoes (fresh and sun dried), prunes, celery, parsley, lemon, garlic, onion, salt, ginger, cinnamon and cayenne. Add 1/2 avocado and blend. Pour into serving bowl.

⇒ Sprinkle top of soup with chopped tomato, parsley, avocado, red pepper, and pine nuts.

SWEET & SOUR SAUCE

Great as a dipping sauce for Nori Rolls or for veggies.

Extra Prep Time: None
Quantity: 1 1/4 cups

Ingredients:
- 2/3 cup dates (measure after removing dates)
- 1/2 cup lime juice (or 1/4 cup lime juice and 1/4 cup lemon juice)
- 1/4 cup olive oil
- 1 tablespoon apple cider vinegar
- 1 tablespoon fresh ginger (chopped)
- 1 teaspoon sea salt
- 1 tablespoon beet (optional--added for colour)

⇒ Blend all ingredients. Store in the fridge. Sweet & Sour Sauce will stay fresh for a week.

THAI CARROT COCONUT SOUP

A delightful soup with lots of flavour and colour.

Extra Prep Time: None
Quantity: 3 1/2 cups

Ingredients:
- 1 1/2 cups water (if too thick, add another 1/2 cup)
- 1 1/2 cups carrots (cut in 2" chunks), or fresh carrot juice
- 1 green onion
- 1/2 of a lemon (not peeled if organic)
- 1 tablespoon dates (measure after pit removed)
- 5 tablespoons fresh or dried coconut (shredded, unsweetened)
- 1 teaspoon turmeric
- 2 tablespoons fresh lemongrass (finely chop the heart of 2 stalks)
- 1 tablespoon fresh ginger (chopped fine)
- 1/2 teaspoon sea salt
- 1 avocado - half (to blend) & half cut in 1/2"- 3/4" pieces (for topping)
- 2 tablespoons fresh cilantro (chopped for topping)

⇒ Blend all ingredients, except avocado and cilantro until smooth. Add half avocado and blend. Pour into serving bowl.

⇒ Sprinkle top of soup with avocado pieces and chopped cilantro.

VANCOUVER ISLAND DRESSING

Vancouver Island Dressing can be prepared in a blender, but you'll miss out on the interesting texture the food processor gives it.

Extra Prep Time: None
Quantity: 2 cups

Ingredients:
- 3 medium carrots
- 1 tablespoon raisins
- 2 tablespoons lemon juice
- 3 garlic cloves
- 1 medium tomato
- 1/3 cup fresh parsley
- 1/3 cup fresh dill
- 1/2 teaspoon sea salt
- 2 dashes cayenne
- 1 avocado

⇒ In a food processor, process carrots, raisins, lemon juice and garlic until carrots are small bits.

⇒ Add rest of ingredients to food processor and process until creamy, but tiny bits of carrots are still visible. Store in the fridge. Vancouver Island Dressing will stay fresh for a few days.

ALTERNATIVE:
Use 1 teaspoon Italian spices instead of the fresh dill.

CHAPTER 5 - APPETIZERS, CRACKERS, SALADS, ENTREES

On a raw food diet, the definition of appetizers, salads and entrees isn't as distinct as with cooked foods. A salad might be the entree. Stuffed Mushrooms, Guacamole, Pizza or Salsa could be appetizers or entrees. Therefore, I'll let you decide whether you're having an appetizer, salad or entree (with crackers on the side). Bon Appetit!

AMAZING AVOCADOS

This recipe is so simple to make and uses ingredients you probably have on hand. Amazing Avocados, served on sprouts, are a popular item at ZenZero-Raw Food Oasis, here in Courtenay, British Columbia.

Extra Prep Time: None
Quantity: lunch for 1 person

Ingredients:
- 1 tablespoon lemon juice
- 1 garlic clove (pressed)
- 1 green onion (finely chopped)
- 1/4 teaspoon sea salt
- pinch of cayenne
- 1/4 to 1/2 teaspoon curry powder (or 1 tablespoon fresh cilantro)
- 1/2 cup carrots (grated)
- 1 avocado
- sprinkle of paprika (optional)

⇒ Put the lemon juice, garlic, green onion, salt, cayenne and curry powder in a bowl. Stir in the carrots.

CONTINUED ON NEXT PAGE

AMAZING AVOCADOS CONTINUED:

⇒ Carefully cut the avocado in half, lengthwise. Scoop the inside of the avocado into the bowl with the rest of the ingredients. Save the avocado shells. Slice the avocado until the pieces are 1/4" to 1/2" chunks....don't mash the avocado.

⇒ Spoon the mixture into the avocado half shells to serve. Sprinkle paprika on top as a garnish (optional).

⇒ Eat just like that, or:
   - on sprouts, or spread on crackers
   - rolled in a nori sheet, or on a lettuce leaf
   - on veggies such as sliced carrots, red pepper chunks, celery
     sticks, jicama slices, daikon radish slices

ASPARAGUS & RED PEPPER SALAD

Extra Prep Time: - Prepare Ginger Sauce (see recipe).
                 - Tastes better marinated for one hour or more.

Quantity: 2 1/2 cups

Ingredients:
- 3 tablespoons Ginger Sauce (see recipe – also tastes good using apple
  cider vinegar instead of lemon juice)
- 1 1/2 cups thin asparagus (cut off tough ends & discard; cut stalk
  in 1" pieces)
- 1 cup red pepper (chopped)

⇒ Prepare Ginger Sauce, which needs no extra prep time.

⇒ Place all ingredients in serving bowl and stir gently to coat. Can be served immediately, but it's better if marinated for 1 hour or more in the fridge.

CAN'T BEET THAT SALAD

This is one of my favourite salads and it's so easy to make.

Extra Prep Time: None
Quantity: 1 3/4 cups

Ingredients:
- 2 medium beets (peeled and grated)
- 1 1/2 tablespoons apple cider vinegar
- 1/8 teaspoon sea salt
- 1 avocado (cut in 1/2" to 3/4" pieces)

⇒ Combine beets, vinegar and salt in a bowl.

⇒ Gently stir avocado pieces into beet mixture.

CARROT QUINOA SALAD

Extra Prep Time: Soak quinoa for two to three hours, then sprout for eight to twelve hours.

Quantity: 3 1/2 cups

Ingredients:
- 1/3 cup dry quinoa (to soak and sprout)
- 2 cups carrots (peeled and grated)
- 1 tablespoon raisins
- 2 tablespoons lemon juice
- 1 tablespoon fresh cilantro or parsley (chopped)
- 1/2 teaspoon sea salt
- dash of cayenne
- 1 avocado (cut in 1/2" to 3/4" pieces)

⇒ Soak quinoa for two to three hours.

⇒ Drain quinoa in a fine mesh strainer and rinse several times. To sprout a tail, leave quinoa in the strainer for eight to twelve hours, covered with a damp cloth.

⇒ In the serving bowl combine all ingredients, except the avocado.

⇒ Add avocado pieces to bowl and stir gently.

CHILI CRACKERS

These crackers are very tasty, without being too spicy. I love the fermented flavour, which also provides beneficial bacteria. Thin crackers can be a replacement for chips. Thick crackers can be used to make sandwiches.

Extra Prep Time: - Leave dough out for one to two days to
ferment (or use lemon juice instead).
- Dehydrate for eight to ten hours.

Quantity: 4 sheets (12" x 12")

Ingredients:
- 2 cups whole brown flax seeds
- 2 cups water
- 1/4 cup raisins
- 2 garlic cloves
- 1 medium onion
- 2 celery stalks
- 2 tablespoons chili powder
- 1/2 cup fresh cilantro
- 1 tablespoon lemon juice (only use if mixture will not be left out to ferment)

⇒ Pour flax seeds in a large bowl (glass, ceramic or metal). I prefer the texture using whole flax seeds, but you can grind half of them.

⇒ Blend the remaining ingredients and stir into the flax seeds. Cover the bowl with a tea towel and leave out for one to two days, stirring the dough each day. Fermentation adds a pleasant sour taste (and good bacteria), so add lemon juice only if you are not fermenting the dough.

CONTINUED ON NEXT PAGE

CHILI CRACKERS CONTINUED:

⇒ Stir dough and spread 1/8" to 1/4" thick on parchment, plastic or teflex dehydrator sheets. Using a spatula, score the dough into the size crackers you want. Dehydrate at 105 degrees.

⇒ When the crackers have been in the dehydrator for five or six hours, flip over onto the mesh dehydrator trays and remove the parchment, plastic or teflex.

⇒ Dehydrate for a total of eight to ten hours (until very dry). To test for dryness, squeeze each cracker - if not firm, dehydrate until dry. When done, allow to cool, then place in a covered container. Crackers remain crunchier if they aren't refrigerated. They will keep well for more than a month if they are very dry.

COLESLAW

Extra Prep Time: None
Quantity: 4 to 5 cups (The cabbage gets soft, which results in the reduced amount of Coleslaw compared with initial ingredients.)

Ingredients:
- 6 cups green cabbage (approximately 1/2 cabbage)
- 1 cup carrots (peeled and grated)
- 1/3 cup fresh parsley (chopped)
- 1 teaspoon sea salt
- 1 dash cayenne
- 1 tablespoon olive oil
- 2 to 3 tablespoons apple cider vinegar
- 2 teaspoons raisins (optional)

⇒ Cut the cabbage in half, cutting through the core. Cut one of the halves in half again, and slice off the hard core (unless you like the core). Finely slice the cabbage and place in a bowl.

⇒ Add the remaining ingredients to the bowl and stir gently.

CUCUMBER DILL SALAD

Cucumber Salad is easy to prepare and very flavourful.

Extra Prep Time: None
Quantity: 1 1/2 cups

Ingredients:
- 1 1/2 cups cucumber (thinly sliced)
- 1 tablespoon red onion (thinly sliced)
- 1 tablespoon fresh dill (chopped)
- 2 teaspoons olive oil
- 2 teaspoons apple cider vinegar
- 1/2 teaspoon sea salt

⇒ Place all ingredients in serving bowl and stir gently.

GUACAMOLE

Guacamole is great on its own, or:
- served with Salsa (see recipe)
- on sprouts
- spread on crackers
- rolled in a nori sheet, or on a lettuce leaf
- scooped using crackers or tortilla chips
- scooped using veggies such as sliced carrots, red pepper chunks,
 celery sticks, jicama slices, or daikon radish slices

Extra Prep Time: None
Quantity: 2 cups

Ingredients:
- 2 avocados (diced or mashed)
- 1 tomato (diced)
- 2 or 3 garlic cloves (chopped very fine)
- 1 green onion (finely chopped)
- 2 tablespoons lemon and/or lime juice
- 1 tablespoon fresh cilantro (chopped fine)
- 1/4 teaspoon sea salt
- 1/8 teaspoon cayenne, or finely chopped jalapeno

⇒ Stir all ingredients together in a bowl and refrigerate.

HUMMUS / FALAFELS / RAW WRAPS

Hummus is easy to prepare and can be made into Falafels by dehydrating it. Hummus or Falafels can also be eaten in Raw Wraps.

HUMMUS:

Hummus is great on crackers (see Chili Crackers, Savoury Crackers or Tortilla Chips), or as a dip for Veggies (e.g. broccoli, carrots, cauliflower, celery, cucumbers, jicima, mushrooms, radishes, red peppers, romaine leaves, tomatoes, or zucchini).

Extra Prep Time: - Soak sunflower seeds for four to eight hours
Quantity: 2 1/2 cups

Ingredients:
- 1/2 cup sunflower seeds (to soak)
- 1 medium zucchini (= approximately 2 cups) cut in 1" chunks
- 3 tablespoons olive oil
- 4 tablespoons lemon and/or lime juice
- 3 cloves garlic
- 1 teaspoon sea salt
- 1/2 teaspoon ground cumin
- 1/2 teaspoon curry
- 4 tablespoons sesame seeds (to grind), or 4 tablespoons raw tahini

⇒ Soak sunflower seeds for four to eight hours, then drain and rinse.

⇒ In food processor, process sunflower seeds and all ingredients, except sesame seeds or tahini, until smooth. Add sesame seeds (ground in a coffee grinder), or tahini, and process until combined. Will keep for several days, if refrigerated.

FALAFELS & RAW WRAPS CONTINUED ON NEXT PAGE

HUMMUS/FALAFELS/RAW WRAPS CONTINUED

FALAFELS:

Falafels are made by dehydrating Hummus, with more curry, cumin and sesame seeds added, plus some parsley. They are great eaten alone, or with Ginger Sauce (see recipe), or in Raw Wraps.

Extra Prep Time: - Prepare Hummus using sunflower seeds soaked four to eight hours (see recipe on previous page)
- Dehydrate Falafels approximately nine hours

Quantity: 18 Falafels (2" rounds x 1/4" thick)

Ingredients:
- 2 1/2 cups Hummus (see recipe on previous page)
- 1 tablespoon curry
- 1/2 teaspoon ground cumin
- 1/3 cup dry sesame seeds (to grind)
- 2 tablespoons fresh parsley (chopped)

⇒ Stir curry, cumin, sesame seeds and parsley into Hummus. For each Falafel, place two tablespoons of mixture on parchment, plastic or teflex dehydrator sheets, and flatten patties into 2 1/2" rounds. Dehydrate at 105 degrees.

⇒ After about three hours of dehydrating, Falafels are firm enough to remove from parchment, plastic or teflex sheets, and place on mesh dehydrator trays.

⇒ Dehydrate Falafels for approximately nine hours in total. They are best the first day, but will keep for several days if refrigerated. For traveling, dehydrate approximately twelve hours in total.

RAW WRAPS:

Falafels or Hummus are yummy in Raw Wraps, which start with a red cabbage leaf, or lettuce leaf holding a Falafel, or Hummus. To this add a slice of tomato, slices of red pepper and Ginger Sauce (see recipe). If using a Falafel in the Raw Wrap, add tomato, red pepper and Ginger Sauce close to serving time so the Falafel doesn't get soggy.

MARINATED MUSHROOMS

Use Marinated Mushrooms for a tasty, quick side dish, on Pizza, or to add zip to soups or salads.

Extra Prep Time: None
Quantity: 2 cups

Ingredients:
- 1 tablespoon raw agave nectar
- 1/4 cup olive oil
- 1/4 cup apple cider vinegar
- 1 1/2 tablespoons Italian spices
- 1/4 teaspoon sea salt
- dash of cayenne
- 12 medium size mushrooms (sliced 1/4 inch thick)

⇒ Place all ingredients, except mushrooms, in a container with a lid that will store the mushrooms. Stir well.

⇒ Add the mushrooms and gently stir to ensure all mushrooms are coated. Store in fridge. Gently turn container periodically so the mixture coats the mushrooms. Marinated Mushrooms will be good for a week in the fridge.

NEATBALLS & NEATLOAF

Neatballs are very satisfying. They are even better with Chili Sauce, Barbeque Sauce or Marinara Sauce (served in a separate dish to keep the Neatballs drier). Neatballs are a great topping for Spaghetti.

Neatloaf uses the same ingredients as Neatballs, plus Barbeque Sauce.

Extra Prep Time: - Soak nuts and seeds approximately eight hours.
- Dehydrate Neatballs four hours, or Neatloaf six hours.
- Prepare Barbeque Sauce for Neatloaf.

Quantity: 30 1" Neatballs, or 4" x 7"x 1" Neatloaf

Ingredients:
- 1/2 cup almonds (to soak)
- 1/2 cup sunflower seeds (to soak)
- 1/2 cup pecans (to soak)
- 1 green onion
- 2 celery stalks (cut in 1" chunks)
- 2 tablespoons fresh parsley
- 2 tablespoons olive oil
- 2 tablespoons poultry seasoning
- 1 teaspoon sea salt
- 1/8 teaspoon cayenne, or jalapeno (chopped very fine)
- 1/4 cup flax seeds (to grind)
- 2 cups Barbeque Sauce (see recipe) if making Neatloaf

⇒ Soak almonds, sunflower seeds and pecans for approximately eight hours. Drain and rinse. In a food processor, process well with the other ingredients, except flax, and place in a large bowl. Add ground flax seeds to the bowl and mix well.

⇒ For Neatballs: Roll the mixture into 1 1/4" balls (dehydrating will shrink them to 1" balls) and place directly on mesh dehydrator trays. Dehydrate at 105 degrees approximately four hours—until the outside is dry.

NEATLOAF CONTINUED ON NEXT PAGE

NEATLOAF CONTINUED

⇒ <u>For Neatloaf:</u> Form the mixture into a 4" x 7"x 1" loaf on parchment, teflex, or plastic dehydrator sheet. Push edges straight using a spatula. Dehydrate at 105 degrees for five hours, then remove from parchment, teflex, or plastic and place directly on mesh dehydrator tray. Spread one cup of Barbeque Sauce on the top of the Neatloaf. Put the other cup of sauce in a small serving dish to serve with the Neatloaf. Dehydrate the Neatloaf and the Barbeque Sauce in the serving dish for an hour.

NORI ROLLS

Nori Rolls are nice served with Sweet & Sour Sauce and Pickled Ginger (see recipes) . I love eating Nori Rolls with chopsticks!

Extra Prep Time: None
Quantity: 12 - 14 pieces

Ingredients:
- 2 nori sheets (dried, not roasted or toasted)
- 1 avocado
- 1 celery stalk (cut the full length of each stalk in 4 strips, but you only need 2 of the 4 strips)
- 1 green onion (chopped fine)
- 1/2 cup carrots (grate, then stir in 1/2 teaspoon lemon juice)
- 1/2 cup red pepper (cut in thin, long strips)

⇒ Lay nori sheets on a dry surface. The ingredients are only put on half of the nori sheet so that they end up in the middle of the roll.
  - Spread half an avocado on each sheet (squishing the avocado with a fork works well).
  - Put a celery slice on each sheet, letting the celery stick out each end of the sheet. Besides being tasty and crunchy, the celery slice will make it easier to roll the sheet later.
  - Add the green onion, then carrots and red pepper, letting some red pepper stick out the ends of the sheet.

⇒ Roll each sheet snuggly, starting with the half of the nori sheet that has ingredients on it. Moisten the end of the sheet with water or lemon so it will stick to form a Nori Roll. Allow closure to dry for a few minutes, then cut in one inch pieces using a sharp knife, or a serrated knife. Stand each piece on the cut so you can see the ingredients.

CONTINUED ON NEXT PAGE

NORI ROLLS CONTINUED:

Variations of Nori Rolls:

- Instead of the avocado, use Sunny Spread or Veggie Pate (see recipes). If Veggie Pate is very moist, add ground sesame seeds, ground sunflower seeds or chopped sundried tomatoes.

- Add sunflower sprouts. They're tasty and nutritious, plus Nori Rolls are attractive with sprouts sticking out the ends.

- Add fresh herbs such as dill or fennel.

- Adding daikon radish will look like rice. Peel the radish, then cut 4" strips using a julienne peeler or a vegetable peeler.

- Add grated yams (peeled) instead of carrots.

NORI SNACKS – CURRY/ITALIAN/SAVOURY

Nori Snacks are very tasty, chewy and great to take on hikes. They can be eaten without dehydrating, but need to be dehydrated to keep for more than a day.

Extra Prep Time: - Soak nuts and seeds for four to twelve hours.
- Dehydrate Nori Snacks for one to three hours.

Quantity: 9 snacks (each 6" long), or 18 snacks (each 3" long), using 1 cup of mixture

Ingredients (Here are a few types to try):

CURRY NORI SNACKS:
- 1/4 cup almonds (to soak)
- 1/2 cup sunflower seeds (to soak)
- 1 1/2 teaspoons apple cider vinegar
- 1 1/2 tablespoons dates (remove pits before measuring)
- 1 teaspoon curry
- 1/4 teaspoon sea salt
- 3 nori sheets (dried, not roasted or toasted)

ITALIAN NORI SNACKS:
- 1/2 cup sunflower seeds (to soak)
- 1/4 cup sesame seeds (to rinse in a strainer; don't grind)
- 1 tablespoon sun dried tomatoes
- 1 teaspoon lemon juice
- 1 1/2 tablespoons dates (remove pits before measuring)
- 1 teaspoon Italian spices
- 1/4 teaspoon sea salt
- dash cayenne
- 3 nori sheets (dried, not roasted or toasted)

CONTINUED ON NEXT PAGE

NORI SNACKS CONTINUED:

SAVOURY NORI SNACKS:
- 1/2 cup sunflower seeds (to soak)
- 1/4 cup pumpkin seeds (to soak)
- 1 tablespoon apple cider vinegar
- 1 1/2 tablespoons dates (remove pits before measuring)
- 1 1/2 teaspoons curry
- 1/2 teaspoon cumin
- 1/2 teaspoon fresh ginger
- 1/4 teaspoon sea salt
- 3 nori sheets (dried, not roasted or toasted)

⇒ Soak almonds eight to twelve hours; sunflower and pumpkin seeds four to eight hours; just rinse sesame seeds.

⇒ Drain and rinse nuts and seeds. In a food processor, process all ingredients, except the nori sheets.

⇒ Nori sheets are approximately 6" x 8". Using scissors, cut each sheet in three strips which are each 6" long. Lay these nine nori sheets flat on a dry surface. Spread the mixture on half of each nori sheet so that the mixture will end up in the middle of the roll, when the sheet is rolled. Roll each sheet snuggly, starting with the half of the nori sheet that has ingredients on it. Moisten the end of the sheet with a bit of water or lemon so it will stick to form a Nori Snack. If you want to make 3" long Nori Snacks, allow the closure to dry for a few minutes, then cut each Nori Snack in half using a sharp knife, or a serrated knife.

⇒ Dehydrate Nori Snacks directly on mesh dehydrator trays (not on parchment, plastic or teflex sheets) at 105 degrees. Dehydrate a total of one to three hours, depending on how dry you want the Nori Snacks. They will be good for several weeks if they are fairly dry and stored in the fridge.

ORIENTAL SALAD

Besides being colourful, Oriental Salad is very tasty, and has delightful textures. Have fun eating it with chopsticks.

Adding arame (a sea weed) is optional; however, it's an interesting and beneficial addition to your diet. Read the description on the label because some companies steam their arame, which makes it not raw.

Extra Prep Time: - None
Quantity: 4 cups

Ingredients:
- 1/4 cup dried arame (a sea weed) to soak in a cup of water (optional)
- 2 tablespoons apple cider vinegar
- 3/4 teaspoon sea salt
- dash of cayenne
- 3/4 teaspoon fresh ginger (chopped)
- 2 teaspoons raisins
- 2 cups carrots (peeled, then grated)
- 1 cup bean sprouts
- 1/2 cup grated: celery root (peeled), or parsnip (peeled), or zucchini (not peeled)
- 2 tablespoons cilantro (chopped)
- 1 cup greens (chopped), preferably dark green
- 1 avocado (cut in 3/4" to 1" chunks)

⇒ Arame is an optional addition to this salad. To soften the arame, soak it in a cup of water while you prepare the rest of the salad.

⇒ Place the vinegar, salt, cayenne, ginger and raisins in the serving bowl and stir.

⇒ Add the rest of the ingredients and stir gently.

⇒ Drain and rinse the soaked arame, then stir into the rest of the salad.

PICKLED GINGER

Pickled Ginger is usually served with Nori Rolls. It can also be added to salads, soups, sauces or seed cheese for some zip.

Extra Prep Time: - Marinate for an hour or longer
Quantity: 1/2 cup ginger

Ingredients:
- 1/4 cup raw agave nectar
- 1/4 cup apple cider vinegar (unpasteurized)
- 1/2 cup ginger (use a vegetable peeler to peel, then thinly slice)

⇒ Pour agave and vinegar in a glass jar and stir well.

⇒ Add ginger slices to the jar, making sure ginger is covered with the liquid. Put the lid on the jar and refrigerate. Allow to marinate for an hour or longer. Keeps for more than a month in the fridge.

ALTERNATIVE:
This is an easier way to make Pickled Ginger. Note that it seems to bring out a stronger ginger flavour than the recipe above. Instead of serving thin slices of ginger, the ginger is in small bits which can be spooned onto Nori Rolls, or your plate. You don't need to peel the ginger or slice it thin. Just put the agave and vinegar in a food processor and process with sliced, unpeeled ginger until the ginger is small bits. Store in a glass jar in the fridge.

PIZZA CRUST/CRACKERS

Extra Prep Time: - Soak sunflower seeds for four to eight hours.
- Dehydrate large crusts for eight to twelve hours; small crusts for six to ten hours.

Quantity: 15 x 6", or 25 x 3" or 60 x 1 3/4"

Ingredients:
- 1 cup dry sunflower seeds (to soak)
- 1 cup whole brown flax seeds (to grind)
- 1 tablespoon raisins
- 1 tablespoon lemon juice
- 1/4 cup water
- 3 cloves garlic (chopped a bit)
- 3 green onions
- 1/2 cup celery (cut in 1 inch chunks)
- 3 tablespoons Italian spices
- dash of cayenne
- 1 pound carrots (unpeeled if organic, cut in 2 inch chunks)
- 1 medium size beet (unpeeled if organic, cut in chunks)- optional

⇒ Soak sunflower seeds for four to eight hours, then drain and rinse.

⇒ Grind flax seeds in a coffee grinder and pour into a large bowl.

⇒ Process sunflower seeds, raisins, lemon juice, water, garlic, onion, celery, Italian spices and cayenne in food processor until fine.

⇒ Process carrots (and beet). Add to flax mixture, combine well and allow to set for fifteen minutes so the flax will bind the dough together. Form dough into 1/4" thick circles on plastic sheets (a spring-release ice cream scooper makes uniform amounts; a lifter dipped in water helps to press, form and lift the crust without sticking), gently lift and place on mesh dehydrator trays. Dehydrate at 105 degrees until Crust is completely dry--eight to twelve hours total for large and six to ten hours total for small.

⇒ Allow Crusts to cool, then place in a covered container. Crusts keep well for a month, if not refrigerated.

PIZZAS

This Pizza recipe is a favourite at ZenZero-Raw Food Oasis. You might want to experiment using Marinara Sauce and/or some other toppings (e.g. slices of tomato, garlic, onion, broccoli, avocado),

Extra Prep Time: - Make Pizza Crust (soak seeds four to eight hours, dehydrate six to twelve hours) – can be made weeks in advance.
- Make Barbeque Sauce – can be made days in advance.
- Make Marinated Mushrooms – can be made days in advance, or use fresh mushrooms.
- Sunny Spread (optional) – can be made a day or two in advance.

Quantity: 15 x 6", or 24 x 2 1/2" Pizzas

Ingredients:
- 1 batch of Pizza Crust recipe
- 1 batch of Sunny Spread recipe (optional)
- 1 batch of Barbeque Sauce recipe
- 1 red, yellow or orange pepper (sliced thin, then chopped fine)
- 1/2 cup pitted olives (sliced thin)
- 1/2 batch of Marinated Mushroom recipe or use 6 fresh mushrooms sliced 1/4" thick
- 15 fresh basil leaves (chopped) – optional, but very nice

⇒ Shortly before serving, spread some Sunny Spread (optional) on each Pizza Crust, then Barbeque Sauce. NOTE: If Barbeque Sauce is added too far in advance, the Pizza Crust may get soggy; however using Sunny Spread between the Crust and Barbeque Sauce will keep the Crust dry a bit longer. Top with peppers, olives, mushrooms, then with basil.

ALTERNATIVE:
Put Sunny Spread on Pizza Crust, then top with veggies such as tomato, olives, red peppers and basil.

RAINBOW SALAD

This recipe from Patrick Dubois of Vancouver, British Columbia, is tasty, colourful and easy to prepare!

Extra Prep Time: None
Quantity: 3 cups

Ingredients:
- * kernels cut off 2 cobs of corn (Don't substitute frozen or canned corn. In addition to not being raw, the flavour is different.)
- 1 1/2 cups cherry tomatoes (sliced in half)
- 1/2 cup red onion (sliced thin)
- 1/2 cup fresh basil (chopped fine)
- 1/2 teaspoon sea salt (optional)

⇒ Stir all ingredients together in the serving bowl.

* Kernels can be cut off the cob easier if you cut or break each cob in half. Place the cut end of each cob on the cutting board so that the cob is upright, then slice off the kernels.

RED PEPPER BOATS

My daughter Lisa created Red Pepper Boats. The recipes she likes best are those with minimal ingredients—to really enjoy the flavour of the vegetables. Fill these Red Pepper Boats with cargo and ship them to your mouth.

Extra Prep Time: None
Quantity: lunch for one person

Ingredients:
- 1 red pepper (cut in large wedges)
- 1 avocado (cut in 1/2" chunks)
- 1 garlic clove (bits of garlic sliced extra thin, or garlic from a garlic press)
- 1 tablespoon fresh cilantro or parsley (chopped fine)
- juice of 1 lime
- a few dashes of sea salt

⇒ Put avocado chunks in the red pepper wedges. Add garlic, cilantro or parsley, lime juice and sprinkle with salt.

ALTERNATIVES:
- Use chard or lettuce instead of red pepper.

- Another tasty use of red pepper wedges is to stuff them with raw sauerkraut. A small amount of caraway seeds mixed with the sauerkraut adds a nice flavour.

SALAD IDEAS

Salads provide an abundance of nutrients, are easy to make and taste delicious. Try to vary the ingredients so that you get different minerals and vitamins. Also, eating a variety of foods will help keep you interested in healthy eating habits. Listen to your body's cravings.

Here's one of my favourite salads, followed by some ingredients you may want to substitute or add.

Extra Prep Time: None
Quantity: 3 cups

Ingredients:
- 1 1/2 tablespoons RAW tahini,
   OR 2 tablespoons dry sesame seeds (to grind)
- 1 to 2 tablespoons lemon juice and a bit of grated lemon zest
- 1 tablespoon olive oil (optional because avocado will provide fats)
- 1 tablespoon water – add another tablespoon of water if using ground
   sesame seeds
- 1 or 2 sprinkles of sea salt
- dash of cayenne
- 2 to 3 cloves garlic (crushed)
- 1 1/2 teaspoons Sultana raisins
- 1 tablespoon fresh dill or cilantro (chopped),
   OR 1 teaspoon fresh thyme, basil or rosemary (chopped),
   AND/OR 1/2 teaspoon of a dry spice or herb (e.g. caraway seeds,
   celery seeds, cumin, curry, Italian spices, turmeric)
- 5 sun dried or kalamata olives (soaked in water)
- 1 carrot (grated or julienned, not peeled)
- 1 1/2 cups greens (chopped or torn) – e.g. spinach, lettuce, kale, chard
- 1 avocado (cut in chunks)

⇒ Stir tahini, lemon, oil, water, salt, cayenne and garlic in a bowl.

CONTINUED ON NEXT PAGE

SALAD IDEAS CONTINUED:

⇒ Stir in the raisins, herb and/or spice, olives and carrots.

⇒ Gently stir in the greens so they are evenly coated.

⇒ Add the avocado and stir very gently.

ALTERNATIVES:
- 1 or 2 green onions chopped in 1/4" to 1/2" lengths
- 1 tablespoon parsley (chopped)
- 1 tablespoon dulse (break up whole dulse into 1" pieces)
- 1 teaspoon pine nuts
- 1 or 2 broccoli or cauliflower flowerettes (chopped into 1/4" pieces)
- 2 tablespoons red pepper (chopped)
- 1 teaspoon fresh ginger (unpeeled, finely chopped)
- 1 stalk celery (chopped)
- 1/4 cup cucumber (sliced)
- 1/2 cup fresh tomato (cut in slices) – can also be used instead of lemon juice
- lime juice, orange juice or apple cider vinegar, instead of lemon juice
- 3 sun dried tomatoes (soaked in water or oil for several hours)
- 1 small beet (peeled and grated)
- 2 or 3 mushrooms (sliced)
- 1 to 2 tablespoons whole flax seeds (to grind), or flax seed oil instead of olive oil
- 1/4 cup daikon radish (peeled and sliced), or red radish (sliced)
- 1/4 cup squash (peeled and sliced)
- 1/4 cup turnip (peeled and sliced)
- 1/4 cup zucchini (sliced)
- 1/4 cup celery root (peeled and grated)
- 1/4 cup parsnip (peeled and grated)
- 1 tablespoon hemp seeds
- 1 tablespoon Seasoned Nuts & Seeds (see recipe)

SALSA

The combination of flavours will remind you that this Salsa is still alive!

Salsa is great:
- scooped using Tortilla Chips, Pizza Crackers and/or Savoury Crackers (see recipes)
- served with Guacamole (see recipe)
- served with slices of avocado

Extra Prep Time: None
Quantity: 5 cups

Ingredients:
- 2/3 cup onion (chopped)
- 1 cup fresh cilantro (chopped)
- 2 tablespoons lime juice
- 2 tablespoons raisins
- 1 tablespoon olive oil
- 6 garlic cloves (chopped finely or pressed)
- 1 1/2 teaspoons sea salt
- 1/2 teaspoon cayenne, or 1 teaspoon finely chopped jalapeno
  (or more for Hot!)
- 4 cups fresh tomatoes (chopped)
- 2/3 cup sundried tomatoes (chopped) if fresh tomatoes are juicy.
  The sundried tomatoes will absorb some of the excess juice.
- 1 cup red or yellow peppers (optional – chopped)

⇒ Put all ingredients in a bowl and mix thoroughly. Stored in the fridge, Salsa will remain fresh for several days.

SAVOURY CRACKERS

The three colours of the seeds add to the appeal of these crunchy, flavourful crackers.

Extra Prep Time: Dehydrate eight to ten hours.
Quantity: 4 sheets (12" x 12")

Ingredients:
- 1 cup unhulled sesame seeds (to soak – can also use 1/2 white sesame seeds and 1/2 black sesame seeds)
- 3 cups brown flax seeds (grind 2 of the 3 cups)
- 1 cup golden flax seeds (not ground)
- 2 tablespoons cumin (whole, not ground)
- 1 teaspoon curry powder
- 1 teaspoon sea salt
- 3 cups water
- 1 lemon (include peel if lemon is organic)
- 4 stalks celery
- 1 large onion
- 1 packed cup parsley
- 2 tablespoons raisins
- 1 cup carrots (grated) (optional)

⇒ Soak sesame seeds while preparing other ingredients.

⇒ Place flax seeds, cumin, curry and salt in a large bowl (glass, ceramic or metal) and stir.

⇒ Blend the remaining ingredients except sesame seeds and carrots, then stir into the mixture in the bowl. Drain and rinse the soaked sesame seeds, then stir into the dough. Stir in the grated carrots (optional). Allow to sit for at least fifteen minutes so the flax seeds make the mixture gelatinous.

⇒ Stir dough and spread 1/8" to 1/4" thick on parchment, plastic or teflex dehydrator sheets. Using a spatula, score the dough into the size crackers you want. Dehydrate at 105 degrees.

CONTINUED ON NEXT PAGE

SAVOURY CRACKERS CONTINUED:

⇒ When the crackers have been in the dehydrator for five to six hours, flip over onto the mesh dehydrator tray, and remove the parchment, plastic or teflex.

⇒ Dehydrate for a total of eight to ten hours (until very dry). To test for dryness, squeeze each cracker—if not firm, dehydrate until dry. When done, allow to cool, then place in a covered container. Crackers remain crunchier if they aren't refrigerated and will keep well for more than a month, if they are very dry.

SEASONED NUTS & SEEDS

Have these tasty nuts and seeds on hand when you want something to nibble, or to use as toppings for salads and soups. Try different seasonings—for ideas, refer to Foods For International Flavours (see page 40).

Extra Prep Time: - Soak nuts and seeds for four to twelve hours.
                  - Dehydrate nuts/seeds for about seven hours.

Quantity: 3 cups

Ingredients:
- 2 cups nuts or seeds (to soak) – almonds, hazelnuts, pecans, pumpkin seeds, walnuts, and/or sesame seeds (I like 1 1/2 cups sunflower seeds and 1/2 cup pumpkin seeds)
- 1/3 cup water
- 1/3 cup dates (measure after removing pits)
- 2 tablespoons cinnamon
- 1/2 teaspoon nutmeg
- 1 teaspoon sea salt (optional)

⇒ Soak almonds eight to twelve hours; hazelnuts, pecans, pumpkin seeds, sunflower seeds and walnuts for four to eight hours; just rinse sesame seeds.

⇒ Drain and rinse the nuts/seeds and put in a bowl.

⇒ In a food processor, process the water, dates, cinnamon, nutmeg and salt, then add to the bowl with nuts and seeds. Stir so the nuts and seeds are coated. Spread the mixture on parchment, teflex or plastic dehydrator sheets and dehydrate at 105 degrees for approximately seven hours. After about four or five hours in the dehydrator, use a spatula to turn the nuts and seeds so they dry thoroughly. Allow to cool, then store in a glass jar in the fridge for a month or more.

ALTERNATIVE:
Instead of using cinnamon and nutmeg, add 1 1/2 tablespoons ground cumin and 2 teaspoons curry.

SEEDY SALAD

This is a yummy recipe, plus it uses pulp left over from making Nut Mylk.

Extra Prep Time: To obtain the pulp, make Nut Mylk (see recipe) which requires soaking nuts/seeds for two to twelve hours. Pulp can be prepared the day before, and refrigerated.

Quantity: 9 cups

Ingredients:
- 3 cups nut pulp (see Nut Mylk recipe)
- 1/2 cup apple cider vinegar
- 1/3 cup olive oil
- 1 teaspoon celery seeds
- 1 teaspoon sea salt
- 1/8 teaspoon cayenne
- 2 cups fresh dill (chopped)
- 2 carrots (grated)
- 2 stalks celery (chopped)
- 1 chopped red pepper (optional)
- 1 or 2 avocados cut in chunks (optional)
- 3 cups of greens (lettuce, spinach, kale, etc.)

⇒ Place pulp in a large bowl. Stir in the apple cider vinegar, olive oil, celery seeds, sea salt and cayenne.

⇒ Add dill, carrots, celery, red pepper (optional) and avocados (optional) to the mixture.

⇒ Stir in the greens.

SPAGHETTI / PASTA

Pesto Sauce, or Marinara Sauce (see recipes) are tasty sauces to serve on Spaghetti or Pasta. Serve with Neatballs (see recipe) for the ultimate Spaghetti. Leftover noodles and sauce can be used in salad dressings or soups.

Extra Prep Time: None
Ingredients:
- zucchini, beets, carrots, daikon radish and/or yams
- lemon juice

⇒ Spaghetti "Noodles" can be made by putting zucchini (unpeeled), yams (peeled) and/or beets (peeled) through a Spirooli Slicer, using the strip blade. If a lot of juice comes out of the zucchini noodles, drain noodles in a strainer. If serving both zucchini and beets, prepare the zucchini first and serve it separate from the beets, so that the white part of the zucchini doesn't get red beet juice on it. The Spirooli Slicer cuts one continuous (very long!) strand, so cut the noodles with scissors, or have scissors handy for guests to have fun cutting them as they serve themselves.

⇒ A julienne peeler is another tool for making "Pasta". Use the peeler to cut long, thin strips of carrots (peeled), zucchini (unpeeled) or daikon radish (peeled). A combination of carrots and zucchini is pleasing to look at and to taste.

⇒ Squeeze a bit of lemon juice on the Spaghetti Noodles and Pasta to keep the veggies fresh.

STUFFED MUSHROOMS

Stuffed Mushrooms are a scrumptious finger food to serve at parties or potlucks.

Extra Prep Time: none
Quantity: 2 cups filling for 20 small mushrooms

Ingredients:
- 20 small mushrooms (Stuffed Mushrooms are move flavourful using small mushrooms instead of large ones)
- 2/3 cup pine nuts
- 6 cloves garlic (chopped or pressed)
- 1 packed cup fresh cilantro (chopped)
- 2 tablespoons lemon juice
- 1/2 teaspoon sea salt
- 1/8 teaspoon cayenne
- 1/2 cup red pepper

⇒ Gently wash the mushrooms and twist off the stems. Place the mushrooms on the serving plate and the stems in the food processor.

⇒ In the food processor, process mushroom stems, pine nuts, garlic, cilantro, lemon juice, salt and cayenne until coarsely ground. Place in a bowl.

⇒ Process red pepper in the food processor until it's in small bits. Stir into the pine nut mixture.

⇒ Stuff mixture into the mushroom caps. If there is extra filling, it's great served on crackers. Store in the fridge until ready to serve.

SUNBURGERS

This is always a favourite recipe at my classes. Serve with Barbeque Sauce, or Chili Sauce (see recipes). Can also be served with Better Than Mayo (see recipe).

Extra Prep Time: - Soak sunflower seeds four to eight hours.
                 - Dehydrate patties for four to six hours.

Quantity: 8 full size patties

Ingredients:

Patties: - 1 cup sunflower seeds (to soak)
- 1 teaspoon sea salt
- 1/8 teaspoon cayenne
- 1 teaspoon poultry seasoning
- 3 cups carrots (cut in 2" chunks)
- 1/2 cup celery
- 1/2 cup onion
- 1/4 cup red pepper
- 1 teaspoon fresh parsley
- 1/4 cup flax seeds (to grind)

To Serve: - 8 romaine lettuce leaves
- tomato (sliced to put on patties)
- Better Than Mayo (see recipe) – optional, but oh so good!
- onion (sliced thin to put on patties)
- Barbeque Sauce or Chili Sauce (see recipes)
- thin cucumber slices and fresh dill (optional)

⇒ Soak sunflower seeds for four to eight hours, then drain and rinse.

⇒ In a food processor, process sunflower seeds, sea salt, cayenne and poultry seasoning until well processed. Put in a large bowl.

CONTINUED ON NEXT PAGE

SUNBURGERS CONTINUED:

⇒ In a food processor, process carrots a bit, then add celery, onion, red pepper and parsley until finely chopped. Add to bowl containing sunflower seeds.

⇒ Grind flax seeds, add to mixture and combine well. Form into eight patties, 1/2 inch thick (smaller patties for kids and potlucks). Dehydrate directly on mesh dehydrator tray (without parchment, plastic or teflex sheet) at 105 degrees for four to six hours.

⇒ Serve each patty on the wide portion of a dry romaine leaf (so the leaf can be folded to keep toppings from falling out). Serve tomato, onion, cucumber and dill on a separate plate so patties don't get soggy. Cucumber slices with fresh dill taste similar to pickles.

SUNNY SPREAD

This spread is so easy to prepare and tastes great. I like it on crackers, lettuce, red pepper, cucumber and in Nori Rolls. Try various herbs and spices, and you'll enjoy a different spread each time.

Using Sunny Spread on a Pizza Crust (or a cracker) will keep the Crust drier than putting Sauce directly on the Crust.

Extra Prep Time: Soak almonds and sunflower seeds for approximately eight hours.

Quantity: 1 cup

Ingredients:
- 1/4 cup almonds (to soak)
- 1/2 cup sunflower seeds (to soak)
- 1 teaspoon raisins
- 2 tablespoons apple cider vinegar
- 1 or 2 cloves garlic
- 1/2 teaspoon sea salt
- 1/8 teaspoon cayenne

⇒ Soak almonds and sunflower seeds for approximately eight hours, then drain and rinse.

⇒ Process all the ingredients in a food processor until smooth. Sunny Spread will keep for several days, if refrigerated.

ALTERNATIVES:
Add an herb or spice to Sunny Spread, such as: basil, cilantro, cumin, curry, dill, ginger, Italian spices, oregano, rosemary, or thyme.
- If dried, use 1 to 2 teaspoons.
- If fresh, use 2 to 3 tablespoons.

TABOULEH SALAD

This salad is full of flavour, textures and colour.

Extra Prep Time: Soak quinoa two to three hours, then sprout for ten to twenty hours.

Quantity: 6 cups

Ingredients:
- 1/4 cup dry quinoa (= 3/4 cup sprouted)
- 2 tablespoons lemon juice
- 2 tablespoons olive oil
- 1 teaspoon sea salt
- 1 clove garlic (chopped fine)
- 2 cups fresh parsley (chopped fine)
- 2 cups cucumber (sliced into 3/4" cubes)
- 2 cups fresh tomatoes (sliced into 3/4" cubes)
- 1/3 cup sundried tomatoes (chopped) if fresh tomatoes are juicy. The sundried tomatoes will absorb some of the excess juice.
- 1/2 cup onion (finely chopped)
- 1/4 cup fresh mint (optional – chopped)

⇒ Soak quinoa for two to three hours.

⇒ Drain quinoa and rinse. Place strainer over a bowl and cover strainer with a damp cloth. Allow quinoa to sprout ten to twenty hours.

⇒ Rinse and drain sprouted quinoa. Place quinoa, lemon juice, olive oil, salt and garlic in a serving bowl and stir gently. Add remaining ingredients to bowl and stir gently. Tabouleh Salad can be served immediately, or marinated in the fridge for several hours.

TOMATO SALAD

Tomato salad is simple to prepare and very flavourful.

Extra Prep Time: None
Quantity: 3 cups

Ingredients:
- 3 cups tomatoes (cut in half through the stem, then cut in slim wedges)
- 1/3 – 1/2 cup white onions (very thinly sliced)
- 1/3 cup fresh parsley (chopped)
- 1 teaspoon sea salt
- 2 teaspoons olive oil
- 1 tablespoon apple cider vinegar

⇒ Place all ingredients in serving bowl and stir gently.

ALTERNATIVE:
Tomato Salad is also nice with 3/4 cup red pepper slices added.

TORTILLA CHIPS

Tortilla Chips are great eaten alone, or with Amazing Avocados, Guacamole, Hummus, Pate, Salsa, or dips.

Extra Prep Time: - Soak sunflower seeds for four to eight hours.
- Dehydrate Tortilla Chips for eight to ten hours.

Quantity: 96 Tortilla Chips (2 1/2" x 2 1/2" x 3" triangles)

Ingredients:
- 1 cup sunflower seeds (to soak)
- 1 1/2 cups brown or golden flax seeds, or both kinds (to grind)
- 4 tablespoons lime juice (lemon is also good, but I prefer lime)
- 2 tablespoons dates (measure after removing pits)
- 1 1/2 tablespoons chili powder
- 2 teaspoons sea salt
- 1/2 teaspoon ground cumin
- 3 cups of fresh corn kernels (approximately 4 cobs of corn)
- 1 large onion
- 1 cup red pepper

⇒ Soak sunflower seeds for four to eight hours.

⇒ Lightly grind the flax seeds and put in a large bowl.

⇒ Drain and rinse the soaked sunflower seeds. In a food processor, process the sunflower seeds, juice, dates, chili powder, sea salt, cumin and corn until small bits. Add to the flax in the bowl and stir. Process the onion and red pepper until they are small bits. Stir into the bowl containing the rest of the ingredients.

⇒ Spread the dough on 3 sheets of parchment, plastic, or teflex, so that each sheet has 12"x12" of dough. With the edge of a spatula, score each sheet into 16 squares (3"x3"each), then score each square from one corner to its opposite corner to make triangles. Dehydrate at 105 degrees for four hours, then remove from parchment, plastic or teflex and place directly on mesh dehydrator trays. Dehydrate a total of eight to ten hours, until dry. Cool and store in a covered container in the fridge, or at room temperature, for several weeks.

VEGGIE BITES

Veggie Bites are great finger food for appetizers and potlucks, especially served with Barbeque Sauce, Chili Sauce, Creamy Sesame Dip, Ginger Sauce (my favourite) or Sweet & Sour Sauce.

Extra Prep Time: - Soak almonds and sunflower seeds for approximately eight hours.
- Dehydrate Veggie Bites for nine to ten hours.

Quantity: 24 Veggie Bites

Ingredients:
- 1 cup almonds (to soak)
- 1/2 cup sunflower seeds (to soak)
- 1/2 cup pine nuts (unsoaked)
- 1 1/2 cups carrots (cut in 2" chunks)
- 2 1/2 cups firmly-packed spinach (or other greens)
- 2 tablespoons olive oil
- 2 green onions
- 1 1/2 tablespoons ground cumin
- 1 teaspoon curry
- 1 1/2 teaspoons sea salt
- 1/8 teaspoon cayenne
- 1/2 cup flax seeds (grind the 1/2 cup of seeds)

ALTERNATIVE: use 3 tablespoons poultry spice instead of cumin and curry

⇒ Soak almonds and sunflower seeds for approximately eight hours.

⇒ Drain and rinse almonds and sunflower seeds. Process in food processor with pine nuts until relatively smooth, then place in a large bowl.

⇒ Process the carrots until they are small bits, then add to the bowl.

CONTINUED ON NEXT PAGE

VEGGIE BITES CONTINUED:

⇒ Process remaining ingredients until spinach and onion are small pieces. Stir into the nuts, seeds and carrots.

⇒ For each Veggie Bite, place one tablespoon of mixture onto a parchment, plastic or teflex sheet (a spring-release ice cream scooper is helpful). Form into an oval shape, 1/2" thick (a lifter dipped in water helps to press, form and lift the dough without sticking). Place the Veggie Bite directly on the mesh dehydrator tray. Dehydrate at 105 degrees for a total of nine to ten hours (until relatively firm and the outside is dry). Serve immediately, or allow to cool, then store in the fridge for up to a week.

VEGGIE PATE

Veggie Pate (also called Seed Cheese) can be eaten immediately, or left to ferment. I like a combination of almonds and sunflower seeds. Fermented foods are easy to digest because they are already partially digested by enzymes and healthy bacteria. Serve on red peppers, hollowed-out tomato, lettuce leaves, celery, crackers or just like that.

Leftover Veggie Pate can be dehydrated, similar to Veggie Bites (see recipe). Just add some ground flax seeds so it stays together better, a bit more herbs/spice and perhaps some grated carrots.

Extra Prep Time: - Soak nuts/seeds for four to twelve hours, or use pulp leftover from making Nut Mylk.
- Can be fermented for eight to twenty-four hours.

Quantity: 3 1/2 cups

Ingredients:
- 1 cup nuts and/or seeds (to soak), or 1 cup of pulp from making Nut Mylk. If using sesame seeds, note that they are too small for a food processor to break down. Therefore sesame seeds need to be ground (dry), or blended (see Blender Method on next page), or use sesame pulp from making Nut Mylk.
- 2 stalks celery
- 3/4 cup tomato (or 1/3 cup sundried tomatoes soaked in 1/3 cup of water and the olive oil for about five hours)
- 1/2 cup fresh parsley
- 3 green onions
- 2 teaspoons raisins, or 1 date
- 2 tablespoons olive oil
- 2 tablespoons lemon juice
- 1 teaspoon sea salt
- pinch of cayenne, or 1/4 teaspoon jalapeno
- 1 1/2 teaspoons dry herb/spice OR 2 to 3 tablespoons fresh herbs (e.g. curry, cumin, ginger, dill, Italian spices, basil, rosemary, cilantro, thyme)
- grated carrot or beet, or chopped broccoli, or other veggies

CONTINUED ON NEXT PAGE

VEGGIE PATE CONTINUED:

⇒ Place Nut Mylk pulp in a bowl. If not using leftover pulp, soak almonds eight to twelve hours; hazelnuts, pecans, pumpkin seeds, sunflower seeds and walnuts for four to eight hours. Rinse and drain. If using sesame seeds, grind them or use the Blender Method (see below). Process in a food processor, then place in a bowl.

⇒ Process the other ingredients in the food processor (except for the grated/chopped veggies) and stir into the nuts/seeds. Add grated/chopped veggies. The Veggie Pate is now ready to eat, or can be left at room temperature with a cloth cover for eight to twenty-four hours, to ferment. It will taste stronger the longer it ferments.

BLENDER METHOD:
Finely blend Nut Mylk pulp, or nuts/seeds which have been soaked, drained and rinsed, with 1/3 cup water and the rest of the ingredients (except grated/chopped veggies). Note that sesame seeds should only be soaked for a few hours, or just rinsed and drained. Pour into a nut mylk bag or a strainer, and hang for eight to twenty-four hours with a bowl underneath. The grated/chopped veggies can be added before or after fermenting.

CHAPTER 6 - DESSERTS & SWEET TREATS

Serving fruit for dessert isn't ideal. Fruit digests quickly, especially melons. If you eat food that digests slowly, then eat fruit, the fruit ferments on top of the slower digesting food.

Raw desserts are rich tasting and filling, so they're usually cut in smaller slices than you'd cut a baked dessert.

<u>MAKING RAW PIES:</u>
Raw Pies don't go in the oven, so use some of your fancy and/or interesting plates to prepare and serve. Here's a basic pie recipe:

CRUSTS – Crusts are formed using raw nuts for body and dried fruit to hold it together with sweetness. You can use almonds, coconut, filberts, macadamia, pecans or walnuts. For dried fruit try apricots, dates, figs or raisins.

For a 9" dish, process 2 cups of dry nuts (to soak, or can be left unsoaked) in a food processor until a coarse meal is formed. Add 1 cup of dried fruit to the nuts in the food processor and process. The crust is ready when you can press the dough against the wall of the processor and it sticks. Set aside two tablespoons of the nut/fruit mixture to decorate the top.

FILLINGS – Place 3 cups of sliced fruit on the crust. Process 2 cups of the same fruit with 1 tablespoon lemon juice, 1 teaspoon allspice, and 1/2 cup dried apricots OR 1/2 cup coconut. (Instead of using the apricots or coconut to thicken and sweeten, you can add in 1 1/2 tablespoons psyllium husk at the end of the processing.) Spread over the sliced fruit. (Instead of the processed fruit topping, you can process 2 ripe bananas, 1 tablespoon lemon juice, an avocado and a dash of cinnamon or allspice.) Sprinkle the topping with the nut/fruit mixture that was set aside and refrigerate for at least a half hour to allow it to set.

APPLE CARROT COOKIES

These cookies have a refreshing sweet/sour taste. The texture is crunchy on the outside and chewy inside. You can use leftover nut mylk pulp from making Nut Mylk (see recipe).

Extra Prep Time: Dehydrate cookies for nine to twelve hours.
Quantity: 40 cookies (2" round x 1/3" thick) from 4 cups dough

Ingredients:
- 1 cup dry sesame seeds (to grind), or use 1 cup nut mylk pulp
  from sesame or other nuts/seeds (see Nut Mylk recipe)
- 1/4 cup dry brown and/or golden flax seeds (to grind)
- 1/4 cup raisins (to add whole) + 1/2 cup raisins (to process)
- 1 teaspoon fresh ginger (chopped, not peeled)
- 2 teaspoons cinnamon
- 1 lemon (grate the zest, then juice the lemon)
- 1/4 teaspoon sea salt
- 1 1/2 cups carrots (cut in 2" chunks)
- 2 cups apples (cored, not peeled)

⇒ Put ground sesame seeds (or nut mylk pulp), ground flax seeds and whole raisins in a bowl.

⇒ In food processor, process the other raisins, ginger, cinnamon, lemon zest, lemon juice, sea salt and carrots until carrots are small bits. Add to the bowl containing sesame, flax and raisins.

⇒ Process the apples into small chunks, then stir into the cookie dough. Leave for fifteen minutes to thicken dough. For each cookie, make a 1" ball, then flatten on parchment, plastic or teflex dehydrator sheet so the cookie is 2" wide. Dehydrate at 105 degrees for three to four hours then lift cookies from plastic or teflex onto the mesh dehydrator trays. Dehydrate for a total of nine to twelve hours. Cool and store in a container in the fridge for up to a week.

APPLE PIE

Apple Pie is popular with my students.

Extra Prep Time: - Soak almonds and pecans for approximately
eight hours
- Soak apricots and 1/4 cup dates for up to eight
hours.
- Refrigerate prepared pie for an hour or more.

Quantity: 9" pie

Ingredients:
- 3/4 cup almonds (to soak)
- 3/4 cup pecans (to soak)
- 3/4 cup dried apricots (preferably unsulphured - to soak)
- 1/4 cup dates (to soak), plus 3/4 cup dates (unsoaked)
- 1 cup water (to soak apricots and 1/4 cup dates)
- 1 tablespoon cinnamon
- dash of sea salt
- juice and grated zest of 1 lemon
- 5 medium size apples (cored, but not peeled)

⇒ Soak almonds and pecans in water approximately eight hours. In
another bowl soak apricots and 1/4 cup dates in 1 cup water for up to
eight hours.

⇒ Drain and rinse the almonds and pecans. Don't drain the soaking
water from the apricots and dates.

⇒ Process almonds and pecans in food processor. Set aside 1 tablespoon
of these processed nuts to decorate top of pie.

⇒ Add unsoaked dates to the almonds/pecans in the food processor
and process well. Press the mixture into a 9" round plate.

CONTINUED ON NEXT PAGE

APPLE PIE CONTINUED:

⇒ In the food processor, process the soaked apricots and dates (including soak water), cinnamon, salt, grated lemon zest and lemon juice. Add half of the apples to the mixture and process until apples are small bits. Put in a bowl.

⇒ Thinly slice the remaining apples using the food processor's slicing attachment, or slice using a knife. Stir the apple slices into the apricot/date mixture.

⇒ Spread the mixture on the crust. Sprinkle top with the processed nuts that were set aside earlier. Pie sets nicely if refrigerated for an hour.

BANANA CAROB COOKIES

These cookies are scrumptious and have a great chewy texture. See below for the nut-free alternative.

Extra Prep Time: Dehydrate cookies for 20 to 24 hours.
Quantity: 60 cookies or 6 cups of dough

Ingredients:
- 4 tablespoons shredded coconut (unsweetened)
- 2 cups pecans (unsoaked)
- 10 medium bananas (ripe)
- 1 teaspoon allspice
- 4 tablespoons raw carob powder
- 3 tablespoons lemon juice, plus grated zest of 1 lemon

⇒ Place coconut in a bowl.

⇒ Process pecans in a food processor. Add to the coconut.

⇒ Process bananas, allspice, carob powder, lemon zest and juice until bananas are relatively smooth with some small lumps. Stir into the coconut and pecans in the bowl.

⇒ For each cookie, drop one tablespoon of dough onto a parchment, plastic or teflex sheet. Dehydrate at 105 degrees. After seven or eight hours of dehydrating (when cookies are firm enough not to ooze through the mesh trays), lift cookies from parchment, plastic or teflex to mesh dehydrator trays.

⇒ Dehydrate for a total of 20 to 24 hours (until the cookie is a bit chewy, but the outside is dry). Allow to cool, then store in the fridge for up to a week.

NUT-FREE ALTERNATIVE (Ingredients for 80 cookies):
- 1 cup shredded coconut (unsweetened)   - 14 medium bananas (ripe)
- 1 teaspoon allspice   - 3/4 cup raw carob powder
- 3 tablespoons lemon juice, plus grated zest of 1 lemon

BANANA LEMON PIE

This is the all time favourite dessert in my classes and anywhere I go. It's also very quick and easy to prepare. I always have some pecans and raisins in the fridge in case I want to make a pie.

Extra Prep Time: None
Quantity: 9" x 9" pan = 6 slices (3" x 4 1/2") or 9 slices (3" x 3")

Ingredients:
- 3 cups pecans or walnuts (unsoaked)
- 1 1/2 cups raisins (unsoaked)
- 4 medium bananas
- juice and zest from 1 1/2 medium lemons
- poppy seeds, blueberries, raspberries, slices of colourful fruit, flowers or sprigs of mint (optional)

⇒ Process nuts in food processor.

⇒ Add raisins to the nuts in food processor and process them until the mixture starts to clump together. Press the mixture into a 9"x9" pan.

⇒ Grate the lemon zest on top of the nut/raisin mix. Juice lemons into a bowl. Slice bananas into the lemon juice; stir gently to coat the bananas with juice. Spread banana slices/lemon juice on the cake.

⇒ Optional: Decorate with poppy seeds, blueberries, raspberries, slices of colourful fruit, flowers or sprigs of mint.

BLUEBERRY SURPRISE

Extra Prep Time: None
Quantity: 24

Ingredients:
- 3 cups pecans or walnuts (unsoaked)
- 1 1/2 cups raisins (unsoaked)
- 1 tablespoon lemon juice
- 24 fresh blueberries

⇒ Process nuts in food processor.

⇒ Add raisins and lemon juice to the nuts in food processor and process them until the mixture starts to clump together. Place the mixture in the fridge for ten to fifteen minutes so that it becomes firmer.

⇒ Remove the processed mixture from the fridge and roll into 1 inch balls. Poke a hole in each ball, put in a blueberry, then cover the blueberry with the mixture. Can be refrigerated for a few days.

ALTERNATIVE: For a quicker method, or if you don't like surprises, just place a blueberry on top of each 1 inch ball instead of putting the blueberry in the center of each ball.

CACAO FONDUE

Cacao Fondue is a quick treat for when you want something special. It's a mouth-watering dip or sauce for strawberries, bananas, dates, grapes, pears and pineapple. Cacao Fondue is also a delectable topping for Ice Creme (see recipe).

Extra Prep Time: None
Quantity: 3 tablespoons

Ingredients:
- 1 tablespoon raw cacao powder (or raw carob powder)
- 1 tablespoon raw agave nectar
- dash of sea salt
- dash of allspice
- 2 teaspoons water
- 1 tablespoon raw tahini
- fresh fruit to dip, or to spread sauce on (e.g. strawberries, bananas, dates, grapes, pears, or pineapple)

⇒ In a small dish, stir together all ingredients, except tahini, until completely combined.

⇒ Add tahini and stir well. If sauce is too thick, add more water.

⇒ Dip fruit in the sauce, or spread sauce on fruit.

CARROT CAKE WITH ICING

Extra Prep Time: - Soak nuts approximately four hours.
- Refrigerate cake for an hour or more.

Quantity: 8" x 8" x 1 1/4"

Ingredients:

<u>CAKE:</u>
- 2 1/2 cup pecans, or walnuts (to soak)
- 1 1/2 cup dates (measure after removing pits)
- 1/2 cup raisins
- 1 tablespoon cinnamon
- 1/2 teaspoon cardamom
- 1/2 teaspoon nutmeg
- 1/8 teaspoon sea salt
- 1 tablespoon fresh ginger (chopped in small bits)
- 4 cups carrots (cut carrots in 1" chunks – then measure 4 cups)

<u>ICING:</u>
- 4 tablespoons raw tahini
- 3 tablespoons raw agave nectar
- 2 tablespoons lemon juice & grated zest from 1/2 of a lemon

⇒ <u>CAKE:</u> Soak nuts approximately four hours. Drain and rinse. Process in food processor until small bits. Set aside 1 tablespoon nuts for topping. Add dates to the nuts in food processor and process until there are no big pieces of dates. Put in a large bowl. Add raisins, cinnamon, cardamom, nutmeg and salt to bowl.

⇒ Process ginger and carrots in the food processor until very fine, then add to bowl. Combine well. Pat dough on serving plate forming an 8" x 8" x 1 1/4" square. Push edges straight using a spatula.

⇒ <u>ICING:</u> Put ingredients in a cup and stir well until smooth. Spread Icing over top of cake and sprinkle with processed nuts

Refrigerate cake for an hour so it will set, and flavours will combine nicely. Cake will keep well for several days, if refrigerated.

ALTERNATIVE ICING:
- Process 2 ripe bananas with the juice and grated zest of 1 lemon.

CHOCOLATE BROWNIES & FUDGE

Chocolate Brownies are delicious! Note that if the dough is processed too much, it becomes yummy Fudge.

Extra Prep Time: None
Quantity: 5" x 5" (= 25 squares 1" x 1", or 8 rectangles 2 1/2" x 1 1/4")

Ingredients:
CAKE:
- 1 cup pecans (not soaked)
- 2/3 cup dates (measure after removing pits)
- 1/2 cup hemp seeds (not soaked)
- 1/4 teaspoon sea salt
- 1/8 teaspoon allspice
- 4 tablespoons raw carob powder
- 4 tablespoons raw cocoa powder
- 3 tablespoons orange juice

ICING:
- 2 tablespoons raw cocoa powder
- 1 tablespoon water
- 1 teaspoon raw agave nectar

⇒ **CAKE:** Process pecans in food processor until they are small bits. Set aside 1 teaspoon of processed pecans to use for topping. Add dates, hemp seeds, sea salt and allspice to the pecans in food processor. Process until there are no large pieces of dates; the pecans and dates should be in small bits. NOTE: The dough becomes Fudge if processed too much.

⇒ Add carob, cocoa and orange juice to the mixture in the food processor and process briefly. Press the dough on a plate, making it 5"x5" and 1" thick. Pressing the sides with a spatula helps make the edges straight.

⇒ **ICING:** In a cup, stir the Icing ingredients until thoroughly combined. If too thick, add a bit more water. Spread this thin layer on top of the Brownie or Fudge, then sprinkle with the pecan bits set aside earlier.

Refrigerate for at least fifteen minutes so the Brownie or Fudge will be firmer and easy to cut. Store in the fridge in a covered container.

DEHYDRATED BANANAS

As mentioned in the 'Is It Raw?" section, most dried fruits sold in stores are dried at high temperatures and often have sulphites and/or sugar added. Banana chips are normally made from unripe banana or plantain slices, with sulphites added before they are fried in oil. Sun-dried fruits are raw. Although it's best to eat fresh fruits, dried fruits come in handy for traveling and for a treat. You can dehydrate your own fruits at temperatures up to 105 degrees Fahrenheit (40.6 Celsius). This recipe makes scrumptious dehydrated bananas. It takes about 24 hours to dehydrate them, if you can resist eating them while they're dehydrating.

Extra Prep Time: Dehydrate approximately 24 hours.
Quantity: as many bananas as you want

Ingredients:
- ripe bananas (bananas are ripe when there are brown spots on the yellow peel)

⇒ Peel each banana, break it in half, then gently squeeze each half. Each banana half will separate into three sections. Place each piece directly on a mesh dehydrator tray (not on parchment, plastic or teflex sheet).

⇒ Dehydrate at 105 degrees for approximately 24 hours. Let the bananas cool. Dehydrated Bananas keep for several weeks, if refrigerated.

DATING AN AVOCADO

Janette Murray-Wakelin, Co-owner of ZenZero, came up with this yummy combination. Dating An Avocado is a super simple snack.

Extra Prep Time: None

Quantity: breakfast, lunch, snack or dessert for one or two people (depends on your appetite)

Ingredients:
- 1/3 cup dates (measure after removing pits)
- 1 ripe avocado
- dash of sea salt (optional)

⇒ Chop dates in 1/2" pieces.

⇒ Cut the avocado in half lengthwise and remove the pit. Put chopped dates in the middle of each avocado and sprinkle with salt. Use a spoon to enjoy your dates with the avocado. That's all there is to it!

DEHYDRATED BANANAS

As mentioned in the 'Is It Raw?" section, most dried fruits sold in stores are dried at high temperatures and often have sulphites and/or sugar added. Banana chips are normally made from unripe banana or plantain slices, with sulphites added before they are fried in oil. Sun-dried fruits are raw. Although it's best to eat fresh fruits, dried fruits come in handy for traveling and for a treat. You can dehydrate your own fruits at temperatures up to 105 degrees Fahrenheit (40.6 Celsius). This recipe makes scrumptious dehydrated bananas. It takes about 24 hours to dehydrate them, if you can resist eating them while they're dehydrating.

Extra Prep Time: Dehydrate approximately 24 hours.
Quantity: as many bananas as you want

Ingredients:
- ripe bananas (bananas are ripe when there are brown spots on the yellow peel)

⇒ Peel each banana, break it in half, then gently squeeze each half. Each banana half will separate into three sections. Place each piece directly on a mesh dehydrator tray (not on parchment, plastic or teflex sheet).

⇒ Dehydrate at 105 degrees for approximately 24 hours. Let the bananas cool. Dehydrated Bananas keep for several weeks, if refrigerated.

FRUIT CRUMBLE (APPLE, BERRY OR PEACH)

Fruit Crumble is easy to make and everyone loves it! Choose Apple, Berry or Peach using what's in season, or berries from your freezer.

Extra Prep Time: None
Quantity: 9 "X 9 " dish

Ingredients:
ALL CRUMBLES:
BASE: See Variations below for the Apple, Berry or Peach base.

FILLING: Use the following ingredients for all Fruit Crumbles, plus Variations shown below for Apple, Berry or Peach filling:
- 1/3 cup raisins
- 1 tablespoon lemon juice + grated zest from 1/2 lemon
- 1/8 teaspoon sea salt

TOPPING:
- 2 cups pecans (unsoaked)
- 3/4 cup dates (measure after removing pits)

VARIATIONS OF FRUIT CRUMBLE:
APPLE CRUMBLE:
Base: - 3 unpeeled, cored apples (thinly sliced)
Filling: - 2 unpeeled, cored apples
           - 1 tablespoon cinnamon
           - see ALL CRUMBLES ingredients above (raisins, lemon, salt)
Topping: - see ALL CRUMBLES ingredients above (pecan, dates)

BERRY CRUMBLE (Blackberry, Blueberry, Raspberry or Strawberry):
Base: - 2 cups berries (fresh or frozen)
Filling: - 1 1/2 cups berries (fresh or frozen)
           - 1/2 teaspoon allspice
           - see ALL CRUMBLES ingredients above (raisins, lemon, salt)
Topping: - see ALL CRUMBLES ingredients above (pecan, dates)

CONTINUED ON NEXT PAGE

FRUIT CRUMBLE CONTINUED:

PEACH CRUMBLE:

Base: - 3 ripe unpeeled peaches (thinly sliced)
Filling: - 2 ripe unpeeled peaches
          - 1/2 teaspoon allspice
          - see ALL CRUMBLES ingredients above (raisins, lemon, salt)
Topping: - see ALL CRUMBLES ingredients above (pecan, dates)

⇒ Place Base in a 9"x9" serving dish.

⇒ In a food processor, process the Filling portion of fruit with raisins, lemon juice and zest, spice and salt until relatively smooth. Stir this mixture into the base fruit in the serving dish and spread evenly.

⇒ For the Topping, process pecans until they are bits. Add dates to food processor and process until dates are small. Sprinkle over the fruit mixture in the serving pan.

FRUIT ROLLUPS

This is a great way to use extra fruit. Fruit Rollups are tasty, fun to chew on and are good for hikes and traveling. You can even use this method of dehydrating when you have too much Smoothie or Soup. Instead of rolling it, you can break it in pieces to munch on, or to use as toppings for salads and soups.

Extra Prep Time: Dehydrate eight to ten hours
Quantity: 1 1/2 to 2 cups of blended fruit on a 14"x14" teflex sheet
produces eight 3"x 6" Fruit Rollups

Ingredients:
- 1 1/2 to 2 cups washed fruit with seeds removed (e.g. apples, apricots, bananas, berries, grapes, mangos, nectarines, papayas, peaches, pears, pineapples, plums, rhubarb – try different combinations of fruit, leaving the peel on fruits such as apples, apricots, grapes, nectarines, peaches, pears and plums)
- 1/8 to 1/4 teaspoon of allspice, cinnamon, cloves, ginger or nutmeg (optional)

⇒ Blend the fruit. You may need a bit of water to get the blender started. Remember that Fruit Rollups will need less dehydrating if no water is added.

⇒ Pour and spread on parchment, plastic or teflex sheet, making the outer edge thicker than the middle because the outside will dry faster. Dehydrate at 105 degrees.

⇒ Depending on the wetness and thickness of the fruit, after eight to ten hours of dehydrating, peel the fruit from the parchment, plastic or teflex sheet (the fruit should still be pliable and easy to peel). Using scissors, cut in strips approximately 3"x 6", then roll up the strips so they are 6" long. Store in a cookie jar or glass container in a relatively cool place; they will retain more flavour if refrigerated. Fruit Rollups keep for several weeks.

GINGERBREAD BALLS

The taste of Gingerbread Balls reminds me of old fashioned gingerbread cookies.

Extra Prep Time: None
Quantity: 20 balls (1 1/4 inches)
Ingredients:
- 2 cups sunflower seeds (not soaked)
- 3 tablespoons fresh ginger (chopped)
- 1 tablespoon cinnamon
- 3/4 teaspoon ground cloves
- dash of sea salt
- 1 cup dates (measure after removing pits)
- 1 tablespoon lemon juice

⇒ Process sunflower seeds, ginger, cinnamon, cloves and sea salt until seeds are very small. Put 2 tablespoons of processed mixture in a small bowl to coat balls.

⇒ Add dates and lemon juice to the mixture in the food processor. Process until mixture is smooth and starts to clump together.

⇒ Squeeze and roll into 1 1/4" balls. Coat with the seed mixture set aside in the first step.

⇒ Store in the fridge for maximum freshness. Gingerbread Balls keep well for weeks.

ICE CREME

Besides being better for you than dairy or soy ice creams, Ice Creme is a delicious creamy treat. It can be served as a parfait by alternating layers of Ice Creme and some fruit in an individual serving glass. For pizzazz, drizzle with Cacao Fondue, or sprinkle top with a dash of cinnamon or allspice.

Extra Prep Time: - Freeze the banana for at least twelve hours.
                  - If using dried fruit, soak for one hour or more.

Quantity: 1 1/2 cups

Ingredients:
- 1 medium size banana (*frozen – see methods below)
- 3 tablespoons dates, dried apricots <u>or</u> figs (soaked in 3 tablespoons water, <u>or</u> 1 tablespoon lemon juice / 2 tablespoons water / grated zest of half a lemon),
  <u>OR</u> 1/3 cup fresh or frozen berries,
  <u>OR</u> 1/3 cup fresh apricot, mango, nectarine, orange, peach, pear <u>or</u> plum
- dash of sea salt
- 1/8 teaspoon cinnamon or allspice (optional)
- 1 teaspoon flax oil, <u>OR</u> 1/2 an avocado (optional – extra creamy)

⇒ Two methods to freeze the banana:
  1) Peel the banana and put in a container in the freezer. This method makes the frozen banana easy to use; however sometimes the banana turns brown if the freezer isn't super cold.
  2) Put the whole unpeeled banana in the freezer. To use, rinse the frozen banana with lukewarm water, then cut off the peel. This method is quick to put in the freezer and the banana won't turn brown, however cutting off the frozen peel can be a chilling experience (great way to cool off!).

⇒ If using dried fruit, soak for one hour or more. If using frozen berries, take out of the freezer ten minutes before using so they can defrost slightly. Also, remove the banana from the freezer ten minutes before using and cut in 1" chunks.

CONTINUED ON NEXT PAGE

ICE CREME CONTINUED:

⇒ In a food processor, process the fruit (not the banana), salt and cinnamon or allspice (optional). If fruit isn't very juicy, add a small amount of water. Add oil or avocado (optional) and process. Add banana and process, but don't over-process or it will be runny rather than creamy. If runny, freeze for about 15 minutes or more. Serve right away or freeze. Will keep for several days, if frozen, although best if eaten when first made.

LEMON POPPY SEED ENERGY BALLS

Perfect food to take on hikes or travelling. Also try Gingerbread Balls, Cinnamon Energy Balls and Licorice Energy Balls.

Extra Prep Time: None
Quantity: 18 balls (1 1/4 inches)

Ingredients:
- 1 cup sunflower seeds (not soaked)
- 1/4 cup pumpkin seeds (not soaked)
- 1/4 cup sesame seeds (not soaked)
- 1/4 cup shredded coconut (unsweetened)
- 4 teaspoons poppy seeds
- 1/4 teaspoon allspice
- 2/3 cup raisins
- 3 tablespoons lemon juice & grated zest from half a lemon

⇒ Process sunflower seeds, pumpkin seeds, sesame seeds, coconut, poppy seeds and allspice until seeds are very small. Put 2 tablespoons of processed mixture in a small bowl to coat balls.

⇒ Add raisins, lemon juice and lemon zest to the mixture in the food processor. Process until raisins are small and mixture starts to clump together.

⇒ Squeeze and roll into 1 1/4" balls. Coat with the seed mixture set aside in the first step.

⇒ Store in the fridge for maximum freshness. Energy Balls keep well for weeks.

MINI PECAN PIES

Mini Pecan Pies are so yummy and easy to make. Serve as hors d'oeuvres, or treat yourself when you have a craving for something sweet.

Extra Prep Time: None
Quantity: as many as you want
Ingredients:
- Medjool dates
– pecans (unsoaked) – 2 pecans for every date

⇒ Cut Medjool dates in half (not lengthwise) and remove the pits.

⇒ Put a pecan in each date half. That's it!

ALTERNATIVE:
Use almonds instead of pecans. Almonds are best if soaked for eight to twelve hours, then drained and rinsed.

ORANGE SESAME CHEWIES

Orange Sesame Chewies are cookies with a nice chewy texture.

Extra Prep Time: Dehydrate cookies for approximately ten hours.
Quantity: 40 cookies (2 1/2" round)

Ingredients:
- 3/4 cup unhulled sesame seeds (to soak)
- 1/4 cup brown flax seeds (to grind)
- 3/4 cup water
- 3/4 cup dates (measure after removing pits)
- 1/2 teaspoon sea salt
- 5 oranges (If organic: peel oranges & add 1 tablespoon of peel.
      If orange isn't organic: peel oranges & add 1/2 teaspoon allspice.)
- 1 cup carrots (grated)

⇒ Soak sesame seeds in some water while you prepare the rest of the
   ingredients.

⇒ Grind flax seeds and put in a large bowl.

⇒ In a blender put the water, dates, salt, oranges and orange rind (or
   allspice). Drain and rinse the soaked sesame seeds and add to the
   blender. Blend the foods that are in the blender until fairly smooth,
   then stir into the bowl containing flax seeds.

⇒ Grate carrots and stir into the mixture. For each cookie, drop 1
   1/2 tablespoons of dough onto the parchment, plastic, or teflex
   dehydrator sheets. Smooth bumps so the cookie is approximately
   3" wide. Dehydrate at 105 degrees. After approximately six hours
   of dehydrating, lift cookies from parchment, plastic or teflex onto
   the mesh dehydrator trays. Dehydrate for a total of approximately
   ten hours (don't dry thoroughly like you would crackers), then cool.
   Orange Sesame Chews will keep for several weeks, if refrigerated--
   unless someone raids the cookie jar ☺. They don't need refrigeration,
   but will stay fresher longer in the fridge.

PUMPKIN PIE

Be sure to include Pumpkin Pie in your menu for Thanksgiving.

Extra Prep Time: Ideal if pie is refrigerated for an hour or more.
Quantity: 9" round plate = 10 - 12 slices

Ingredients:

CRUST:
- 2 cups pecans (not soaked)
- 1/2 cup dates (measure after removing pits)
- 2 teaspoons cinnamon
- 1 teaspoon nutmeg
- dash of sea salt

FILLING:
- 4 cups pumpkin (peeled, seeds removed, cut in 1" chunks)
- 1 tablespoon water
- 2/3 cup dates (measure after removing pits)
- 1 tablespoon cinnamon
- 1 teaspoon nutmeg
- 1/2 teaspoon cardamom
- 1/4 teaspoon ground clove
- 1/4 teaspoon allspice
- dash of sea salt
- 4 tablespoons coconut butter (left in a warm area to soften)

ICING:
- 1/2 cup raw cashews (see page 31 – Is It Raw?)
- 1/2 cup dates (measure after removing pits)
- 1 orange (peeled)
- 1 tablespoon water or orange juice

PIZAZZ:
- can use 2 tablespoons of the Crust or:
- 1 tablespoon raw cacao powder (optional)
- 1 tablespoon raw agave nectar (optional)
- 2 teaspoons water (optional)

CONTINUED ON NEXT PAGE

PUMPKIN PIE CONTINUED

⇒ <u>CRUST:</u> Process pecans in food processor. Add dates, cinnamon, nutmeg and salt to the pecans in food processor, then process until smooth. If you are not decorating the pie with the cacao powder, agave nectar and water, set aside 2 tablespoons of Crust to use for Pizzazz. Press the rest of the Crust into a 9" round plate.

⇒ <u>FILLING:</u> In food processor, process pumpkin and water until smooth. Add dates, cinnamon, nutmeg, cardamom, cloves, allspice, salt and coconut butter and process until smooth. Spread on the Crust.

⇒ <u>ICING:</u> Put cashews, dates, orange and water in a blender and blend until smooth. Spread on the Filling.

⇒ <u>PIZAZZ:</u>
- If you <u>won't</u> be decorating with cacao, agave and water, sprinkle the Icing with the 2 tablespoons of Crust you set aside earlier.
- If you <u>will</u> be decorating with cacao, agave and water, stir them together in a small container until smooth. Using a spoon, drizzle on top of the pie in whatever pattern you want.

Refrigerate for an hour or longer to firm up. Pumpkin Pie remains yummy for several days, if refrigerated.

SAUCY FRUITS

Pat Newson, a fantastic raw food chef, found that blueberries processed with date soak water, thickens like a pudding. Pectin in fruits combines with the sugar in dates to act as a natural thickener. Enjoy Saucy Fruits just like that, or drizzled over cakes, pies or Ice Creme.

Extra Prep Time: None
Quantity: 3/4 cup

Ingredients:
- 1/3 cup dates (measure after removing pits)
- 1 tablespoon water
- 1 tablespoon lemon juice
- 1 cup fruit (apple, apricot, blueberries, nectarine, plums, peach, pear, pineapple or strawberries)
- 1/2 teaspoon allspice, nutmeg or cinnamon

⇒ Process dates, water and lemon juice in a food processor.

⇒ Add the fruit and spice to the date mixture in the food processor. Process until smooth or fruit is small bits (depends what you want). Refrigeration for an hour or more will thicken Saucy Fruits.

TRUFFLE FRUIT PIE

This pie will satisfy chocolate lovers. The pears (*or strawberries, raspberries, kiwis or mangos) nicely round out the flavour and texture.

Extra Prep Time: Allow pie to set for a half hour or more.

Quantity: 9" x 9" plate = 9 - 12 slices

Ingredients:

CRUST:
- 2 cups pecans (unsoaked)
- 1/4 teaspoon sea salt
- 2/3 cup dates (measure after removing pits)
- 4 tablespoons raw cacao powder
- 4 tablespoons raw carob powder

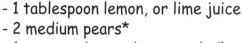

FRUIT SLICES:
- 1 tablespoon lemon, or lime juice
- 2 medium pears*
  (quartered, cored, not peeled)

FILLING:
- 1/2 cup coconut butter (left in a warm area to soften)
- 1/2 cup dates (measure after removing pits)
- 3 tablespoons lemon, or lime juice
- 1/4 teaspoon sea salt
- 1/4 teaspoon allspice
- 2 medium pears* (quartered, cored, not peeled)
- 2/3 cup raw cacao powder (or cacao and carob)

PIZAZZ:
- 1 tablespoon shredded coconut (optional – for contrast)
- 10-15 mint leaves (optional – adds delightful taste & colour)

⇒ CRUST: Process pecans and salt in food processor. Add dates to the pecans in food processor, then process until smooth. Add cacao and carob, then process. Press onto a 9" x 9" plate (round or square).

⇒ FRUIT SLICES: Squeeze juice into a bowl. Thinly slice pears into juice and gently stir to coat them. Leave 1/3 of the most attractive slices to decorate the top of the pie; arrange the rest on crust.

⇒ FILLING: In food processor, process coconut butter, dates, juice, salt, allspice and pears until small bits. Add the cacao powder and process until relatively smooth. Spread on the fruit slices.

⇒ PIZAZZ: Arrange fruit slices around the top edge, sprinkle coconut in the middle and arrange mint leaves between coconut and fruit.

Refrigerate pie for at least a half hour to firm it up.

TRUFFLES

Truffles taste so decadent, yet are easy to make.

Extra Prep Time: None
Quantity: 15 truffles (1" balls) or 24 smaller truffles (3/4 " balls)

Ingredients:
- 1 cup pecans (not soaked)
- 1/2 cup dates (measure after removing pits)
- 1/4 teaspoon sea salt
- 4 tablespoons raw carob powder, plus 1 tablespoon for coating
  (or use half raw carob powder and half raw cacao powder)
- 1 tablespoon shredded coconut (unsweetened)

⇒ Process pecans in food processor. Set aside one tablespoon of the processed pecans in a small bowl for coating some truffles.

⇒ Add dates, salt, carob/cacao to the pecans in food processor. Process until mixture is smooth and able to clump together when squeezed.

⇒ Put the remaining tablespoon of carob/cacao in a small bowl. Put the shredded coconut in another small bowl.

⇒ Roll the processed mixture into balls. Coat some of the balls in the processed pecans, others in the carob/cacao and the rest in shredded coconut. For the balls that are coated with processed pecans, sometimes I like to roll them in carob/cacao after their pecan coating. Store in the fridge for several weeks or in the freezer for a month.

ALTERNATIVES:
- For another scrumptious, yet easy treat, slice a banana into a bowl and crumble two or three Truffles on it.

- If you are fortunate enough to have raw mesquite powder, try using it instead of raw carob powder. I like half raw mesquite powder and half raw cacao powder

- Add 3 tablespoons goji berries (not soaked) to process with the pecans.

CHAPTER 7 - HEALTHY LIFESTYLE MORSELS

Eating healthy food significantly impacts our vitality. You probably already know that smoking, drinking coffee or soda, eating sugar, artificial sweeteners, white flour and white rice aren't good for our health. Here's some information about other lifestyle changes that can improve your quality of life.

BREATHING

Usually we don't give much thought to breathing...it just happens. As a result, many people don't breathe very deeply. Sometimes when I'm in a place where the air is clean, I inhale for four seconds, then exhale for five to six seconds. I repeat this several times to get the stale air out of my lungs and to give my body more oxygen. When you're faced with a challenging situation, taking a few deep breaths can help provide clarity.

FASTING

Fasting is not ingesting anything except water. It's something all animals do when they're not feeling well because it's such a natural way of healing. Digestion uses a lot of our energy, so if we fast and rest, our body can devote it's attention to cleansing and healing. During a fast it's best to keep warm, and rest in bed or a comfortable chair. Stretching and short walks help blood and lymph circulate, to remove toxins. Calm music and audio books make time pass more enjoyably. Blood pressure is usually lower during a fast, which can result in dizziness...put your head between your knees. Walk and stand up slowly. Drink about six to eight cups of pure water, such as reverse osmosis water. Some days water will taste good and others it won't. Your tongue will probably be coated for most of the fast, which is a sign that toxins are being eliminated. You can brush your tongue with a wet toothbrush. Keep a journal regarding your cleansing reactions, weight, water intake and thoughts for reference.

For the first two days of the fast your body burns glucose. By the third day, glucose is out of your system, so the body switches to burning fat reserves , where most toxins are stored.

Coming off a fast should be followed by a gradual reintroduction of solid foods (follow a ten day water fast with five days of adding foods). Eat very small amounts of fruit for the first day, chewing completely to stimulate peristaltic action in the digestive system. The taste of food is incredible! Following with a raw food diet is ideal.

Some people choose to do a juice fast because they can continue most of their normal activities. Note that the body is still receiving nutrients, so it never burns fat reserves as the primary source of fuel and less detoxification occurs. Dr. Joel Fuhrmann, in his book *Fasting and Eating For Health* states that *"Juice fasts and severely restrictive diets cause us to lose more lean body tissue and less fatty tissue than do total fasts."*

If you have a lot of stored toxins, you may want to start cleansing by eating more raw foods, including Green Smoothies, with a water fast later on. Read about fasting until you feel comfortable enough to do it on your own, or go to a fasting specialist for a supervised fast. I fasted on my own for ten days, after a lot of reading and discussions with people who had done a number of water fasts. I found it interesting that on the third day of the fast I smelled like potato chip oil from all the potato chips I had eaten in the past. I've heard of mechanics who smell like gasoline during a fast--years after they had stopped working as mechanics. Fasting is powerful.

KAGEL EXERCISE

This is a simple exercise if you have trouble with incontinence (including leaks when you sneeze, cough or laugh). For women, besides strengthening the bladder muscles, it also has the pleasant side effect of tightening muscles around the vagina.

Tighten the pelvic floor muscles as if you're trying not to urinate, and attempt to hold it for ten seconds. Some people refer to it as the elevator exercise because you can visualize an elevator going up when you tighten your muscles, then down when you release. You can do this anywhere. I prefer the following method: Sitting on the toilet, I urinate a bit, then do the Kagel Exercise for ten seconds, then urinate, then Kagel Exercise again for ten seconds. Doing it this way, I can tell whether my bladder muscles are strong enough to hold back the urine.

After I had my second child, I had trouble holding my urine until I reached the washroom. I did Kagel Exercises several times a day. The first day of exercise it felt like nothing was happening, but doing it several times a day over the course of a week, my bladder muscles were able to hold back the flood. Now I do Kagel Exercises when I feel my bladder muscles aren't allowing me as much time to get to the washroom as I'd like. (I realize this info is getting rather personal, but I wanted to share it with you in case you had the same problem.)

LESS CLUTTERED LIVES

Many of us shop for entertainment. Our possessions can weigh us down. Besides the initial monetary investment, we invest our time cleaning, moving, sorting and walking around things. Some possessions hold us back emotionally because they remind us of unpleasant times. Before making a purchase, I often figure out how many hours I need to work to pay for the item. I shop at thrift stores, but need to watch that I'm not bringing clutter home just because it's a good price.

I became more aware of the true cost of possessions when I moved from Ontario to British Columbia. I was moving from a three bedroom home with a basement and garage, to a small apartment, so I had to get rid of a number of things or put them in storage. I knew that I'd be making a few more moves in my lifetime, which would require my money and energy to move the items. Giving things to friends and charity became a very freeing experience.

In Vancouver I met a woman who was comfortably living on less than $8,000 per year. I was amazed because I was earning $50,000 and was in debt. I started reading about living simply and it struck a cord. The media has a huge impact on our spending habits, making us want things we don't really need, and, perhaps can't afford.

LYMPHATICS & EXERCISE

Our lymphatic system carries waste materials from our cells. It's similar to the blood system, except that it depends on movement to move lymph, rather than having a pump, like the heart. Deep breathing, exercise, massage, skin brushing and sweating are all ways to make lymph move. Many detox symptoms are the result of high concentrations of toxins. If our lymphatic system is flowing well, detoxification reactions are reduced.

Years ago people didn't need to do exercise because their lives were filled with movement and physical labour. It's great if you're one of those people who are active in sports. If not, you might try some simple activities like walking, riding a bike or even parking your car at the end of the parking lot. You can do some light exercises like stretching, bending and sit-ups. Yoga, Tai Chi and Qi Gong are all relaxing and beneficial. Besides being good for the Lymphatic system, exercise helps us de-stress.

Skin brushing removes dead skin and wastes that clog pores, and stimulates blood and lymph circulation. Brushing with a dry natural fiber brush should be done on dry skin before showering. Use long gentle strokes towards the heart. Lymph accumulates in the lymph nodes, so brush those areas first (the armpits and the groin are locations of some lymph nodes), using a circular motion, so the lymph can flow more freely.

When I feel symptoms of a cold, sore throat, or earache, there are usually lumps on the sides of my throat under my jaw. I lightly massage the lumps to loosen the toxins that are sitting in the lymph nodes there. I may also gargle with salt water (half a teaspoon in half a cup of lukewarm water).

Sweating helps eliminate toxins directly through the skin. Saunas are a relaxing way to sweat.

NOURISHING YOUR SKIN & HAIR

Whatever you put on your skin gets absorbed by your body. I try not to put anything on my skin that I wouldn't be willing to eat. Read labels. If you have trouble pronouncing a word, there's a good chance you shouldn't be using it on your skin or hair. Here are some natural alternatives that probably cost less than products on the shelf.

ALOE VERA – An aloe vera plant is good to use for rashes, sunburn or eczema because it soothes and stops itches. Just slice off a piece of the plant, cut it open and apply the gel directly to the area. Aloe vera gel really helped me when I had extremely itchy rashes from a latex allergy.

APPLE CIDER VINEGAR (unpasteurized)– Use full strength as a compress to reduce swelling and pain, and accelerate healing. Pour it on gauze, put on the inflamed area and cover with plastic wrap. Don't use ice because it freezes cells and prevents healing. For a soothing bath, add two cups apple cider vinegar to the water.

AVOCADO – The oil in avocado is a good moisturizer. Apply part of a ripe avocado to your face and/or body. Enjoy a moisturizing facial mask: gently massage two tablespoons of avocado into your skin, leave on for five minutes or more, then rinse with warm water.

COCONUT OIL – I use organic unrefined coconut oil as my face moisturizer and for dry spots on other parts of my body. Apply small amounts so the skin doesn't get saturated and have a greasy film. Coconut oil is wonderful for massages. Also, my cats have shiny coats because they each love licking a 1/4 teaspoon of coconut oil off my finger every day.

COMPLEXION BRUSH – Instead of using soap or cleansers on my face, I splash on some warm water, then gently rub a complexion brush in circles on my face and neck, avoiding the eye area.

DEODORANT – When I stopped using a deodorant, I rubbed a piece of lemon or put apple cider vinegar under my armpits to kill bacteria. Now I rarely use anything (and it's safe to be downwind of me).

EYE COMPRESS – For irritated and/or puffy eyes, apply a compress using chamomile tea. Steep chamomile in very warm water for fifteen to thirty minutes, then pour through a strainer. The tea can be kept in a jar in the fridge for several days. Pour some cooled tea on a face cloth, lay back and relax, with the face cloth on your eyelids. I found it very soothing when my eyes were puffy and itchy from seasonal allergies. Sometimes I just wet two chamomile tea bags and put them on my eyes. I stored them in the fridge to use again within a few days.

FLAX SHAMPOO/SHAVING CREAM/SOAP – Debby Boyes, a dear friend who passed away, inspired many raw fooders to use flax seeds as the base for shampoo, shaving cream and as soap. The oil in flax leaves hair and skin soft, with no need for a conditioner or to apply lotion after a shave. Finely grind two tablespoons of dry flax seeds in a coffee grinder, then pour in a container you can keep in the shower. Add 3/4 to one cup water and about five drops of an essential oil such as lavender or peppermint. Put a lid on the container and shake it. The mixture will thicken in an hour. I don't refrigerate the mixture, so I make a new batch each week. If my hair is oily, I rub my hair with some lemon juice or apple cider vinegar before using the flax shampoo.

FLEA PREVENTION ON CATS OR DOGS – Instead of using a flea collar, flea shampoo or giving your companion animal a drug for fleas, you can add nutritional yeast to food. Fleas dislike the flavour and will avoid your cat or dog. Use about a teaspoon of nutritional yeast daily for cats and small dogs, and a tablespoon for a fifty pound dog. They love the taste of it added to their food. During peak flea season, double the amount of nutritional yeast. Some animals are yeast intolerant and will react with a skin allergy. Stop using it if that happens. Nutritional yeast isn't a raw food, but it's definitely better than the chemical based options.

GINGER – Adding fresh ginger to Smoothies, Juices or other foods helps inflammation, swelling and indigestion.

OLIVE OIL – This is good to use as a moisturizer. Don't use too much on your face, or your face will look too shiny.

PAPAYA – The papaya's juicy orange flesh can be used for skin rejuvenation. Rub the inside of a papaya's skin on your skin, to moisturize and aid healing.

PARSLEY – Eating parsley can freshen your breath and it's a diuretic. It tastes great added to a Smoothie.

PINEAPPLE – Pineapple contains bromelain, an enzyme which is an anti-inflammatory; therefore it can be ingested to relieve joint and muscle pain.

TOOTHPASTE – Use one that doesn't contain fluoride. A toothpaste that doesn't contain glycerine helps rebuild enamel.

WATER – Water treated by reverse osmosis is good. Swim in clean natural bodies of water, or in pools that use ozone to clean the water, rather than in chlorinated pools.

OTHER – For your safety and that of the environment, you may want to rethink the use of some of these products: fabric softener, dryer sheets, detergent for clothes, makeup, suntan lotion, cleaning products, perfume and artificial air fresheners.

SLEEP

It's important to get enough sleep, especially when making changes in your life. When we're awake, all of our systems are competing for the available energy. Our body needs to sleep in order to recharge and to repair cells. Once it completes those jobs, it can devote time to getting rid of old toxins stored in our cells. Therefore, if we don't get enough sleep, we won't be as healthy and vibrant as we can be.

Try not to eat two to three hours before going to sleep for the night. When you eat close to bedtime, you may find it harder to fall asleep and your sleep won't be as deep.

I find a fifteen to twenty minute nap very energizing. If the nap is longer than thirty minutes, I usually feel groggy, unless I was extremely tired.

SUNSHINE

Sunshine is important to our well being. Our body needs it to produce vitamin D. We know that lack of sunshine can affect our mood. Try to get at least fifteen minutes in the sun, several times a week.

WHAT MAKES YOUR HEART SING?

Figure out what your passion in life is and go for it! If you're not sure what you want, think back to what you liked to do when you were very young. Just thinking about it may give you a feeling of excitement. Often we get sidetracked from doing something we love and need to rekindle the old feelings we had. There are many books that can help you. Once you open your mind and heart to what makes your heart sing, you'll feel more alive and the answers will come to you.

**Wishing You Much
Health, Love and Laughter
on Your Life's Journey!**

APPENDIX

WELLNESS ASSESSMENT

Complete this Wellness Assessment now, in two weeks, in four weeks and in two months. Watch for and celebrate any improvements!

1. GENERAL **Rate the following from 1 to 10:** **(1 = poor; 10 = great)**	NOW Date:	2 WKS Date:	4 WKS Date:	2 MOS Date:
Ability to Communicate				
Ability to Handle Stress				
Appetite				
Attitude				
Body Tone				
Concentration				
Creativity				
Energy Level (am)				
Energy Level (afternoon)				
Energy Level (pm)				
Flexibility				
Intellectual Growth				
Memory				
Quality of Relationships				
Sociability				
Spiritual Growth				
Stamina				

CONTINUED ON NEXT PAGE

WELLNESS ASSESSMENT CONTINUED:

2. ACTIVITIES, HABITS	NOW	2 WKS	4 WKS	2 MOS
How Many Times a Week I Do Each of the Following:				
Argue or Yell				
Crave Sugar or Salt				
Drink Alcohol				
Drink Caffeinated Beverages				
Eat Junk Food				
Eliminate				
Exercise				
Laugh or Smile				
Lose My Temper				
Meditate / Pray / Quietly Reflect				
Remember My Dreams				
Smoke or Chew Tobacco				
Socialize				
Use Drugs (Prescription or Otherwise)				
Wake Up Rested				
Watch TV				
Other (specify)				

CONTINUED ON NEXT PAGE
WELLNESS ASSESSMENT CONTINUED:

3. PHYSICAL CONDITIONS	NOW	2 WKS	4 WKS	2 MOS
Rate from 1 to 10:				
Allergies (1=none; 10=extreme)				
Bacterial or Fungal Infection (1=none; 10=widespread)				
Blood Pressure (1=normal; 10=high)				
Breathing (1=easy; 10=difficult or painful)				
Circulation (1=no problem; 10= cold hands and feet)				
Elimination (1=regular; 10=painful or irregular)				
Equilibrium (1=no dizziness; 10=frequent loss of balance)				
Gastro-Intestinal Upset – gas, heartburn, burps, pain (1=never; 10=constant and painful)				
Gum and/or Tooth Pain (1=never; 10=constant)				
Halitosis (1=never;10=constant)				
Headache(1=never;10=constant)				
Heartbeat (1=regular; 10=irregular)				
Hemorrhoids (1=none; 10=frequent and painful)				
Insomnia/Difficulty Falling Asleep (1=none; 10=nightly)				
Joint Pains (1=never; 10=constant)				
Other: _____ (1=never;10=constant)				

DIARY

Date & Day of Week: _____

Weight: _____

Amount & Quality of Sleep:_____

Time	Activities, Foods, Medications	How I Feel Physically	* How I Feel Emotionally

* Clues for Emotional Imbalance: agitated, anxious, bored, depressed, hyper, irritable, mad, restless, sad, scared, scattered

Clues for Emotional Balance: calm, confident, easygoing, energized, excited, focused, happy, humorous, interested, patient, relaxed

RECOMMENDED READING

There are many health related books and websites. Look for links on my website **www.rawrose.com**. Here is some reading which I highly recommend:

www.rawbc.org, **www.rawfoods.com** and **www.foodnsport.com**

Raw Family, *12 Steps To Raw Foods*, and *Green for Life* by Victoria Boutenko. Also, *Eating Without Heating* by Sergei and Valya Boutenko. The Boutenko's books, website **www.rawfamily.com** and monthly newsletter have a wealth of information. *Is Raw Food for You?* is a great video to introduce or reinspire interest in raw foods.

Raw Secrets, a book by Frederic Patenaude, and his website **www.fredericpatenaude.com** have lots of good information about the raw food lifestyle.

Sign up for Jim Carey's weekly online newsletter about the benefits of raw foods at **www.chidiet.com/news/mvj/**.

Fasting Can Save Your Life by Herbert Shelton has been reprinted many times since the book's first edition in 1964.

Fasting and Eating For Health by Joel Fuhrmann, MD provides good information about fasting.

Diet For A New America (book and video) and *The Food Revolution* by John Robbins provide a look at how our food choices affect our health and the health of the planet.

How I Conquered Cancer Naturally by Eydie Mae Hunsberger tells how she followed Dr. Ann Wigmore's program to eliminate cancer.

Fats that Heal Fats that Kill by Udo Erasmus is a book that has information everyone needs to know about oils.

NOTES